THE Yorkshire DALES
a view from THE Millennium

EDITED BY DAVID JOY
TEXT SELECTED AND INTRODUCED BY COLIN SPEAKMAN
FOREWORD BY HRH THE PRINCE OF WALES

GREAT NORTHERN

THE
Yorkshire
DALES
a view from
THE
Millennium

YORKSHIRE DALES
MILLENNIUM TRUST

Title page photo: Upper Wharfedale from above Conistone, with Kilnsey Crag on the left *(Simon Warner).*

Published by Great Northern Books, Holebottom Farm, Hebden,
Skipton, BD23 5DL

The Yorkshire Dales Millennium Trust, registered charity no.1061687,
receives £1 for every copy sold

Copyright © David Joy, Colin Speakman and Great Northern Books, 1999

ISBN: 0 9535035 3 4

Design, layout and maps: Barry C. Lane, Sutton-in-Craven
Jacket design: Blueprint Marketing Services, Ilkley

The assistance of NORWEB in the publication of this book is
gratefully acknowledged

The publishers are indebted to the following individuals who have
kindly met fees for the reproduction of illustrations:
His Hon. Judge Peter Charlesworth (Bolton Castle and Gayle bridge,
both by Thomas Girtin)
Peter & Victoria Fattorini (Gordale Scar, by James Ward)
Patricia Lennon (Bolton Abbey, by Charlotte Bronte)
Roger Stott (April shower in Wensleydale, by Piers Browne)

Printed on Mediaprint Silk 150gsm manufactured by Stora Enso and
supplied by Benjamin Gough, Leeds
Reproduction and printing: The Amadeus Press Ltd, Huddersfield

Produced with the support of
YORKSHIRE POST

British Cataloguing in Publication Data
A catalogue record for this book is available
from the British Library

Contents

View from Mossdale, North Yorkshire, 1996, HRH The Prince of Wales

I was delighted to be asked to become Patron of the Yorkshire Dales Millennium Trust because I wholeheartedly support the valuable work of this new charity in conserving and enhancing the special qualities of the Dales.

It is splendid that the Trust has chosen to mark the millennium with this book which forms a worthy permanent record and is a remarkable celebration of how the Dales has been portrayed down the ages in prose and poetry, paintings and photography.

With its potent mix of rolling fells, deep valleys, swirling rivers and limestone scars, all bound together by a rich tapestry of drystone walls, the Dales are rightly regarded as one of the most treasured landscapes in Britain. Yet this is also a living landscape, and it is right that this book should focus on such diverse groups as farmers and quarrymen, residents and visitors.

Those who come to the Dales should be under no illusion about the reality of life within the area and the hard work that is expended on maintaining the natural beauty. This beauty does not just happen by chance - it is the result of centuries of continuous management which has created a miraculous partnership between man and nature.

On a recent visit to the Dales I was heartened to see the ways in which farmers are helping to protect the environment. This in turn draws many visitors to the area, thus supporting local incomes and maintaining the viability of services, shops and businesses.

The Trust is forging a new approach to local rural initiatives, helping in the conservation of the Dales and stimulating community life. As its proud Patron, I am greatly impressed by its ability to provide funding and expertise to the small local groups who have ideas and commitment for a wide range of projects.

The Trust is dedicated to ensuring that the special features of the Dales - both its spectacular scenery and its thriving local communities - will enter the new millennium in good heart. I trust that this book will play a part in bringing its aims to a wider public, as well as forming a unique perspective of one of Europe's finest landscapes and its people.

Introduction

Books often evolve in curious ways. This one started with an art exhibition.

The occasion was the golden jubilee in 1997 of the Craven Branch of CPRE (Council for the Protection of Rural England). As its secretary, I had the idea of mounting an exhibition to depict how the Yorkshire Dales had inspired painters over the fifty years of the Branch's existence. Held at The Folly in Settle, its success totally exceeded expectations. Some 200 works were displayed, and at the end of it all there was a feeling that we had paved the way for a broader concept of a more permanent nature.

Hence the vision of marking the year 2000 with a work which would celebrate the area's literary and artistic heritage in the widest sense, showing how the Dales has been portrayed by writers, poets, artists and photographers from early times up to the present day. Nothing in quite the same vein has previously been attempted.

Colin Speakman and I have happily collaborated. Colin has selected the prose and poetry and penned the text 'What makes the Dales so special?' which follows this introduction. I have edited the book, chosen the paintings, drawings and photographs and written the accompanying captions.

This work in no sense pretends to be a review of the last thousand years. For more than half this period the Dales was a cultural unknown, seldom visited and scarcely recorded. Equally it makes no claims to be comprehensive. To do so would need a multi-volume work occupying several feet of shelf space. This is a representative rather than a definitive 'View from the Millennium' and inevitably much of the selection is by personal preference.

The earliest prose extracts are by William Camden, who in 1582 - six years before the Spanish Armada - took in the Dales when he toured England to complete his massive and remarkable work *Britannia*. Poetry begins with William Drayton's verse of 1622, inspired by Giggleswick's Ebbing and Flowing Well. We move forward through the evocative words of Charles Kingsley and Halliwell Sutcliffe to more recent times, when J. B. Priestley, Mike Harding and Bill Bryson are among those who have continued to be captivated by a landscape which inspires such extraordinary affection.

The earliest painting is by Thomas Girtin, about whom Turner made the oft-quoted remark, 'If Girtin had lived I would have starved.' Girtin died in 1802 at the early age of 32 and Turner had few equals when he successfully toured the Dales in 1816. Three outstanding works from this visit are reproduced in these pages.

No book featuring Dales paintings would be complete without James Ward's majestic study of Gordale Scar. Equally fascinating in its own way is Charlotte Bronte's surprisingly little-known drawing of Bolton Abbey, completed in 1833 when all the Bronte children had a day out on the banks of the Wharfe. Among the Victorian artists represented are Atkinson Grimshaw and William Mellor, who preceded an era when the trickle of painters coming to the Dales turned into a flood. Selecting the work of present-day artists has been especially difficult, although the up-and-coming have deliberately been included as well as more established names.

We were especially delighted when HRH The Prince of Wales, Patron of the Yorkshire Dales Millennium Trust, agreed that his painting of Mossdale, a tributary valley of upper Wensleydale, could be reproduced as a frontispiece.

By its very nature the photographic content of this book dates from a later time span than the paintings. No-one really knows when and where the first photograph was taken in the Dales, but by the closing decades of the nineteenth century a brave band of pioneers were following in the footsteps of early artists, lugging their bulky cameras and tripods to the most challenging of locations. Great change came in 1896 when the Post Office permitted picture postcards to be sent through the mail, unleashing a glut of photographic activity which continued unabated until recent times. The amazing factor in retrospect is the minutiae of life depicted on postcards, ranging from sheep washes to stepping stones and from children at play to quarrymen at work.

Another milestone was the launch in 1939 of *The Dalesman* magazine which gave a regular outlet for leading photographers of the day, then still working in black-and-white. We feature two whose work has found good homes: Bertram Unne (his vast collection is now with North Yorkshire County Library) and Geoffrey N. Wright (whose images are in the safe-keeping of the Yorkshire Dales Society).

The advent of colour photography created an even greater explosion of interest in recording the unique attributes of the Dales than had been the case with picture postcards half-a-century earlier. Here we can only skim the surface of a very deep well, reproducing work by John & Eliza Forder (whose photographic books of Dales people were truly pioneering), Geoff Lund (drystone waller turned gifted cameraman) and the outstanding landscape studies of Simon Warner.

One other name deserves specific mention. Marie Hartley is the only person to feature as writer, artist and photographer. For more than fifty years she and Joan Ingilby have collaborated in recording a way of life in the Yorkshire Dales that they could see was rapidly changing. They have been enormously supportive and I am deeply grateful for their help and encouragement.

As a life-long dalesman, it gives me the greatest possible pleasure that this book has been conceived, researched, compiled, designed, marketed and printed in Yorkshire, using materials supplied by a Yorkshire paper merchant. Apart from Colin Speakman, partner in this venture, I would specially like to thank Victoria Fattorini who, as well as proof-reading the text, has also tracked down often elusive paintings in galleries and auction catalogues. As designer, Barry C. Lane has coped patiently with my scribbled visions for the layout of the book. Barry Cox and the team at Blueprint Marketing Services have achieved wonders in many different ways.

Last but not least there is the Yorkshire Dales Millennium Trust. Richard Witt, Director of the Trust, and his colleagues Ann Shadrake, Joanne Darlington, Rebecca Page and Alison Quigley, have all been a source of inspiration in bringing this project to fruition. Many of those who have responded so magnificently in subscribing to this book, as listed on pages 190 to 192, are Trust donors. I hope the result justifies their faith and will prove a worthy 'View from the Millennium'.

David Joy

ACKNOWLEDGEMENTS

Every effort has been made to trace copyright holders in all copyright material in this book. The editor regrets if there has been any oversight and suggests the publisher be contacted in any such event. We gratefully acknowledge the following permissions:

Anna Adams for her poem "The Stone Men".

James Alderson for his poem "Gayle Bannock".

Bill Bryson for "A Favourite View in the World" and "Beautiful Beyond Words", both from *Notes from a Small Island*.

The Bunting Estate for "Spring Journey", from Basil Bunting's *Collected Poems*.

Country Life for "There Must be Dales in Paradise", from *Four Boon Fellows* by A.J. Brown.

David & Charles for "The Story of Malham Mill", from *Old Yorkshire Dales* by Arthur Raistrick.

Peter Gunn for "Easby Abbey", from *The Yorkshire Dales: Landscape with Figures*.

Robert Hale Ltd for "Swaledale's Tide of Colour", from *A Countrygoer in the Dales* by Jessica Lofthouse; "Sunday Afternoon in Malhamdale", from *Portrait of Yorkshire* by Harry J. Scott; and "Bainbridge and its Horn", from *Portrait of the Dales* by Norman Duerden.

Messrs Hamlyn for "The Hiking Craze", from *Moorland Tramping in West Yorkshire* by A.J. Brown.

Mike Harding for "No Chocolate Box Village", from *Walking in the Dales*.

Marie Hartley for "Tan Hill", from *Swaledale* by Ella Pontefract.

Marie Hartley & Joan Ingilby for "A Morning in the Street", from *Yorkshire Village*; also "Shepherds and their Dogs", from *Life and Tradition in the Yorkshire Dales*.

William Heinemann Ltd for "The Escape to the Dales", from *English Journey* by J.B. Priestley.

David Higham Associates for "Darrowby", from *If Only They Could Talk* by James Herriot.

Joan Ingilby for "Haytime", from *Poems by Joan Ingilby*.

W.R. Mitchell for "A Place for Ravens", from *Wild Pennines*.

David Morris for "Keld and its Chapel", from *The Swale - A History of the Holy River of Paulinus*.

Richard Muir for the extract from *The Dales of Yorkshire*.

Frank Peters Publishing Ltd for "The Dalesman", from Arthur Raistrick's introduction to *Open Fell, Hidden Dale*.

Gervase Phinn for "A Child of the Dales", from *The Other Side of the Dales*.

Jean Wright for the use of photographs by Geoffrey N. Wright - and for the extract from *Stone Villages of Britain*.

Darnbrook Cowside, between Arncliffe and Malham - a photograph which arguably could have been taken nowhere else in the world except the Yorkshire Dales. The distant fell contrasts with the green softness of the pasture, and the walls and barn are in perfect harmony. Sheep dotted in the fields are a reminder that this is a fragile landscape, dependent on the continued well-being of upland farming *(Simon Warner)*

A VIEW FROM THE MILLENNIUM

What makes the Yorkshire Dales so very special ?

Colin Speakman

There are few other landscapes in England, perhaps not even in the world, that inspire such intense love and affection. That indefatigable anglophile and traveller, American author Bill Bryson, speaks for many of us when he looks across to the "little lost world" of Malhamdale from the road from Settle past Kirkby Fell and declares that "my favourite view in the world is there."

It could equally have been Swaledale, Dentdale, Wensleydale or Wharfedale. Each of us who know and love the Dales – and that will include most readers of this book – have our own favourite dale, a place which for us is unique and special, where we feel we belong. There are far more spectacular landscapes in the world, in Europe, even in Britain. In the Dales there is perhaps none of the grandeur and majesty of the Scottish Highlands, Snowdonia, or even the Lake District. It is a more intimate landscape. Its special qualities are ones that defy analysis. Some people have suggested that its essential attraction lies in the quite stark contrast between those treeless, eroded uplands, whose summits hold nothing but peat bog, heather moor and wind scoured craggy outcrops, and the green, sheltered softness of the Dales, pasture, drystone walls, scattered farms and woodland, enclosed, almost hidden between those bleak fells.

Other people have claimed that in the Dales, perhaps more than anywhere else in the British Isles, there is a harmony to be found because so much that man has contributed to the landscape is of local materials. Stone walls, barns, bridges, farms, churches and chapels, whole villages seem part of the texture and colour of the landscape. Visually, the natural and man-made in the Yorkshire Dales form an organic whole.

That's where the painters and the photographers have an advantage over the poets and the topographers. They don't need to struggle with those clumsy tools, words, but can record what they see, colours and half tones, that delicate balance between light and shade, between wildness and domesticity, between man and nature, which whilst it is difficult to describe in words, can be understood, communicated through what we see and feel.

It is often claimed that the Yorkshire Dales is a man-made landscape. That's only half true. It wasn't man that caused the vast subterranean movements of the earth's crust that created the great whaleback hills, with dramatic fault lines that reveal those steep escarpments and outcrops; nor the massive glaciers and fast flowing rivers that scoured out the steep valleys; nor the constant gales and frosts that shattered the scars to scree; nor the rains and streams that have scooped out the potholes and

A picture worth a thousand words: a wonderful snapshot of Dales life just a century ago on Grassington Gala Day, June 1900. The procession stretches back up the Main Street as far as the eye can see, unhindered by the motor car which has yet to usher in an era of dramatic change *(Ben McKenzie collection)*

complex labyrinths of caves leaving almost as much of the Dales to explore underground as on the surface.

But mankind has, of course, been a major, and accelerating influence, especially during the Millennium which has just passed. His activities began modestly enough, tribes of hunters, gatherers and early farmers clearing away the primeval forest for primitive homesteads and crofts, draining the marshy valley bottoms, felling but not always replanting timber for fuel and building material, grazing and eventually overgrazing the land to leave those bare, treeless, eroded uplands, and, in relatively recent times, creating the vast sheepwalks, enclosing the land within geometric patterns of drystone walls, cultivating those meadows so rich in flower every

spring, building the scattered barns, the farmsteads that seem indeed to grow out of the hillside, the compact villages, beating out the network of paths and tracks through and across the Dales which for centuries were the only means of communication.

Our species has also been fairly destructive. For centuries, lead mining and stone quarrying destroyed and disfigured the fellside above Wharfedale, Wensleydale, Ribblesdale, Nidderdale and Swaledale, with their shafts and vast spoil tips which a century after the lead and stone mines closed, are still a degradation of the landscape. The quarries, which began as shallow holes for grubbing up building stone and limestone for sweetening the soil, have grown to become massive, intrusive scars on the landscape. In more recent years railways and new roads have turned the Dales from a remote wilderness into a vulnerable paradise, now within a few minutes' travel time of the vast conurbations of modern, technological-industrial Britain. With our massive earth movers, diggers, explosives, pile-drivers, trucks, we can not only quarry away the Dales for industrial limestone, but we could, if we chose, within a couple of decades, transform its still semi-natural landscape into huge commercial forests for wood pulp, reservoirs to feed our unlimited demands for water, wind farms for endless demands for energy, building land for commuter and holiday homes and chalet parks, using any surviving areas in between for ever more artificial mass leisure pursuits of a rich and bored society, such as leisure centres, golf courses, theme parks, helicopter pads, motor sport circuits and bike scrambling areas.

Some of these things have already happened. There are very many people living in and coming to the Dales whose greatest wish in the world is to see many more such things occur in the Dales so that they can benefit financially and politically. Commercial enterprise and activity has its place in the Dales like everywhere else, but unless that activity is of an appropriate scale and unless it is conducted in ways which respect, and protect, that special landscape and cultural heritage, the activity will quickly destroy the very qualities which attract the visitors and the developers in the first place. Each development by itself will not destroy that precious, and increasingly vulnerable, environment, but the cumulative development of each new planning permission, with its new service roads, obligatory large car parks and traffic, will be to degrade and destroy the Dales every bit as certainly and finally as the most massive quarry or open cast mine. It is the risk of what Ken Willson, the first President of the Yorkshire Dales Society, graphically described as "Death by a thousand Cuts."

But the reason why the Dales have not actually, so far, been destroyed is largely due to a relatively small number of people whose feeling and concern for the Dales landscape has so far prevailed against the destroyers.

This book is a tribute to those men and women whose vision, perception and understanding have helped us to appreciate and value what we enjoy today, and a celebration of that achievement. As vital as the work of the legislators of countryside protection and the administrators of what is now the Yorkshire Dales National Park and Nidderdale Area of Outstanding Natural Beauty has been, and as important as the work of the voluntary bodies who have pressured, lobbied and worked to create and support the National Park has also been, the safeguarding of this unique landscape really began around 250 years ago – just a quarter of the Millennium whose passing we celebrate – when the first writers and painters began to discover and appreciate the special qualities of what we now know as the Yorkshire Dales. It was a revelation that this hitherto inaccessible and poverty stricken part of the central Pennines was somewhere worth visiting and therefore ultimately worth protecting.

In a very real sense, we still see the Dales through the eyes of those poets, guidebook writers, painters, and more recently photographers and television directors who have influenced the way we see this landscape and how we feel for it. Enjoying, understanding, appreciating, having feeling for a landscape are something, whilst they are natural enough, that have to be learned, and are determined, not only by our senses, but the culture within which we live.

Mountain and moorland landscapes like those of the Yorkshire Dales were not regarded as particularly beautiful or interesting at least until sometime in the middle of the 18th century. Daniel Defoe, early 18th century journalist and novelist, in his celebrated *Tour Through England and Wales* of 1724, when he looked across to the Dales from the Vale of Lune, could only describe the hills he saw as "all barren and wild, of no use or advantage to either man or beast".

What caused a change of taste and perception by the mid 18th century is difficult to define, but it roots lay in the birth of what most cultural and literary historians would describe as the Romantic movement. Its origins in turn lay in a taste for the curious and the bizarre, the "Gothick" of castles, crags, dark caves and cataracts – all of which the Dales have in abundance – with their hint of nameless horror and terror, and which provided such a suitable contrast to the serene logic but sometimes sterile platitudes of the Augustan Age of Reason. A celebrated account by a clergyman in the *Gentleman's Magazine* of March 1761 of an ascent of Ingleborough (page 61), has all the sense of strangeness and awe which might accompany a description of an ascent of Everest in the

Thomas Girtin (1775-1802), regarded as one of the greatest of early English watercolourists, was also one of the first painters to visit the Dales. His study of Gayle bridge, Hawes, has the added interest of recording the long-vanished leet which supplied water to the village mill *(Birmingham Museums & Art Gallery)*

By mid-Victorian times artists were depicting the Dales as a haven of escape from the new industrial surroundings of nearby towns and cities. Atkinson Grimshaw's painting of Ghyll Beck, Barden, in spring 1867 has been hailed as 'a veritable hymn to nature' with its peaty banks, moss-covered tree trunks, icy waters and early primrose bravely flowering *(Sotheby's)*

1990s, and might properly be described as the moment tourism in the Yorkshire Dales began.

The great and famous soon came by coach and carriage to discover this unknown land of the strange and and curious. When the poet Thomas Gray came to Gordale (page 50) to experience the "horror" of the looming crags and waterfalls he stayed there a full quarter of an hour and thought his trouble richly paid "for the impression will last for life". The very word "picturesque" was – and is – used to describe a view – waterfall, mountain, cottage with shepherd – which artistic taste decreed appropriate to adorn a young lady's album or gentleman's parlour wall.

The Yorkshire Dales, so rich in Caverns and Potholes, very nearly acquired the name Cave District for such was the fame of such places as Weathercote Cave and Alum Pot among the artists and writers who came from all over Britain on still wretched roads by horse and on foot to share in the sense of wonderment at the grotesque and unknown. A taste for the sublime, shaped by such remarkable writers and artists as Thomas Pennant, Edward Dayes, JMW Turner, and perceived as an almost moral force of nature by such figures as William Wordsworth and John Ruskin, became more than a fashion but almost a new nature-worshipping religion.

"Where would the steam boats and railroads now have been leading their passengers"? asked essayist and topographer William Howitt in 1839 were it not for the poets – Bishop Percy, Walter Scott and above all William Wordsworth who set a new agenda for discovering the "mighty power of nature" in the British countryside. By the 1840s the first railways were penetrating the Yorkshire Dales, and the first railway guidebooks – including the first rambling guides – were being written.

But at the same time this was happening, industrialised Britain had created something its newly-rich citizens needed to escape from, the Victorian city. With the rapid expansion of canal and railways, and the steam-powered wool and cotton mills, iron foundries, coal mines and heavy engineering "manufactories" in the towns and cities of Lancashire, West Riding and Teeside, came lung-destroying, black industrial soot, slums, overcrowding and environmental degradation. Owing to ever-increasing competition from the big northern cities, and from abroad, industry in the less accessible Dales was declining. By late Victorian times, the small water-powered mills and the lead mines were closing, Dales communities were migrating in ever large numbers to these new industrial towns or even over "t'girt dub" across the Atlantic to America and Canada.

WHITE ABBEY, LINTON. LIN. 13.

The advent of picture postcards in 1896 was an event comparable with the later invention of the telephone. Photographers had the impetus to portray all aspects of village life - and sometimes recorded the unexpected. This postcard of White Abbey, Linton, depicts the home of Halliwell Sutcliffe, high priest of Dales romantic fiction, who is obligingly sitting in the doorway
(*Ben McKenzie collection*)

But within a couple of decades other people were returning to the Dales, by the railway and motorbus, and later by car, not as workers but as tourists, escaping the polluted and crowded cities for the day or weekend, taking up the increasingly fashionable pastimes of walking, cycling or driving in the countryside. Starved of prosperity, mining villages such as Grassington, Kettlewell or Reeth were still filled with antique, unmodernised workers' cottages which, in the cities would have long been demolished as slums but which, with a few discreet rambling roses around the door, now offered a picturesque retreat. Guidebook writers in the late 19th and early 20th century such as Edmund Bogg of Leeds and Halliwell Sutcliffe were producing popular guidebooks for a newly literate audience, their sentimental descriptions built around a deep nostalgia for a Yorkshire Dales that never was, but largely an invention of their own fertile imagination. Bogg's books were lavishly illustrated by painters and engravers whose work also conveyed a world of lost innocence, far removed from the brutish work of Edwardian Leeds with its manufacturing and commerce where, in Woodhouse Lane, Bogg owned a shop selling books and paintings to an increasingly prosperous bourgeoisie. An image of an idyllic Dales landscape was created to some extent which still persists, especially as reflected in that deep and close bond between the old industrial West Riding and its rural Dales hinterland, which until 1974 was part of the same English county.

To a degree the process continues. Every writer, every painter, every photographer who comes to the Dales – James Herriot and Bill Bryson are just two of the most recent – reinterprets what might be called this Myth of Innocence, presenting an area which is cleaner, purer, more beautiful than urban Britain, with inhabitants who are more honest and likeable than the world outside.

Maybe what we are yearning for, and can sometimes find in the Yorkshire Dales with the help of contemporary writers, poets and painters, is something within ourselves, part of our own identity. Even more than in the last century, modern technology and rapid urban development has transformed the world we struggle to come to terms with. Whole areas of cities and suburbs have been transformed into something unrecognisable, often quite inhuman suburbia with their skyscraper blocks, expressways, traffic jams, concrete, fumes, danger and

A traditional Wensleydale meadow painted by Judith Bromley. Once seemingly threatened with extinction in the cause of increased agricultural productivity, the surviving meadows have now been recognised as a key feature of the Dales countryside to be safeguarded in the new Millennium

above all incessant noise. The Dales offer – at least to some degree – tranquillity, images of a long remembered past which reflect our own roots, our personal family history three or four generations ago, our own origins from a long-vanished rural England, coloured with nostalgia perhaps, but nonetheless real, part of our collective memory, sustaining deeply held spiritual values, reflected in the very language we use, the books we read, the stories we tell our children.

We all need roots. Even if life for most people now living in the Yorkshire Dales, has more in common with life in any prosperous English suburb or commuter village than in the Dales of last century, there is still a farming community in the Dales, whose clipped dialect owes not a little to our Norse, Danish and Anglian ancestors. Hill farming, as a way of life, even with all modern conveniences, still draws back to ancient verities of life, death, the seasons and survival in a harsh and often difficult environment.

And for the visitor (or permanent resident in his or her centrally heated converted farmhouse), this is still an area where, for at least for a day or a weekend, you can leave the trappings of industrial civilisation, including your car, and walk, experiencing, at least for a few hours, this older, perhaps more natural way of life. Like the hill farmer perhaps, you can be in touch with the seasons, the ever changing colour and light, sensing the shape of the land beneath your feet, the sharp feel of wind, rain on your face, the scent of grass or rotting leaves. You can even follow the very same paths and trackways over remote fellsides or along valley heads, in the footsteps of ancestors who, some forty generations ago, were watching the dawn of what to them was the Second Millennium, with a lot more fear and trepidation than we welcome the Third. You can see, give or take a pylon or two, and the odd pebble-dashed bungalow, a landscape which if they returned to earth as sentient shades, they might still be able to recognise.

This book therefore celebrates those interpreters of the Dales landscape – writers, painters, photographers, who have done so much during the last part of the Millennium which has just passed to record the special qualities of the Dales landscape, and to raise our awareness. Much of the material in this book is based on *A Yorkshire Dales Anthology* (Hale) published in 1981 and long out of print. This book not only adds much new written material, but now has a twin focus, contributed by David Joy, including the visual arts – the twin techniques of painting and photography which have contributed so massively to our understanding and appreciation of the Dales. But equally important, the book is not just a backward look "from the Millennium", but looks forward into the next with, in its final section, contributions from a number of young people, now living in the Dales, who have written about or expressed their feelings about the environment and communities within which they live in paint. This material came from a major Painting and Poetry Competition organised in 1999 by the Yorkshire Dales Millennium Trust for schools of the Dales which produced work in both media of outstanding quality. The editor and publishers are grateful to the schools, to the Millennium Trust and to the children for not only taking part in this competition but in allowing us to use the winning entries which, in such a wonderful way, look forward to the Yorkshire Dales in the coming Millennium.

Finally to the Millennium Trust itself. This book, which celebrates the rich cultural inheritance of the Yorkshire Dales, is welcomed by the Trust. A registered charity, the Trust is a mechanism by which conservation of the unique landscape and cultural inheritance of the Yorkshire Dales can become a reality. By working closely with Dales communities, local authorities, parish councils and the National Park Authority, literally hundreds of projects, some large, some small, have been made to happen. They range from small tree and bulb planting schemes, wildlife habitat and wall restoration schemes, to major community projects involving the rebuilding of community halls and education centres, the undergrounding of miles of unsightly electricity cables and the replanting of extensive woodland areas. Whilst the involvement of the Trust's major sponsors has been of vital importance in getting many schemes off the ground, the Trust has also been a way of allowing many thousands of ordinary people to contribute in practical ways to the conservation and in some cases restoration of the Yorkshire Dales.

The Yorkshire Dales is a living, evolving landscape. Its continuation as a source of inspiration and spiritual and emotional renewal for many millions of people not only of the present generation but of many generations to come, will only occur if enough people care sufficiently to ensure that this landscape also enjoys a renewal. Real resources must be found to repair the fabric, to safeguard the wildlife, and to even improve the quality of part of our English countryside which it is the birthright of everyone – visitors and local people alike – to enjoy. Not only will a contribution from the sale of each copy of the book be made to the Trust,, but we hope that the inspiration of those many generations of writers and artists before us, and yet to come, will help to constantly strengthen the resolve of everyone who comes to the Dales, to ensure that this process will continue as the new century and new Millennium unfolds.

Part 1

A Sense of Place

Cray Gill, Upper Wharfedale *(Simon Warner)*

Wharfedale

This *Wharf* or *Wharfe*, in the English Saxon's language *Guerth*, commeth downe out of Craven, and for a while runneth in a parallell distance even with *Are*. If a man should think the name to be wrested from the word *Guer*, which in British signifieth *swift and violent*, verily, the nature of that River concurreth with his opinion; For he runneth with a swift and speedy streame, making a great noise as he goeth, as if he were forward, stubborn and angry; and is made more full and teasty with a number of stones lying in his chanell, which he rollth and tumbleth before him in such sort that it is a wonder to see the manner of it, but especially when he swelleth high in Winter. And verity it is a troublesome River and dangerous even in Summer time also, which I my selfe had experience of, not without some perill of mine owne, when I first travailed over this Country. For, it hath such slippery stones in it that an horse can have no sure footing on them, or else the violence of the water carryeth them away from under his feete. In all his long course which from the Spring head into the *Ouse* is almost fifty miles, he passeth onely by little Townes of no especiall account: running down by *Kilnesey Cragge*, the highest and steepest rocke that ever I saw in a midland Country by *Burnsall*, where Sir *William Craven* Knight and Alderman of London there borne, is now building a Stone bridge: who also hard by, of a pious minde and beneficiall to this Country hath of late founded a Grammar Schoole; also by *Barden-Towre* a little turret belonging to the Earle of *Cumberland*, where there is round about a good store of game and hunting of fat Deere: by *Bolton*, where sometimes stood a little Abbay: by *Bethmesley* the seat of the notable Family of *Claphams*, out of which came John Clapham a worthy warrior, in the civill broiles between *Lancaster* and *Yorke*.

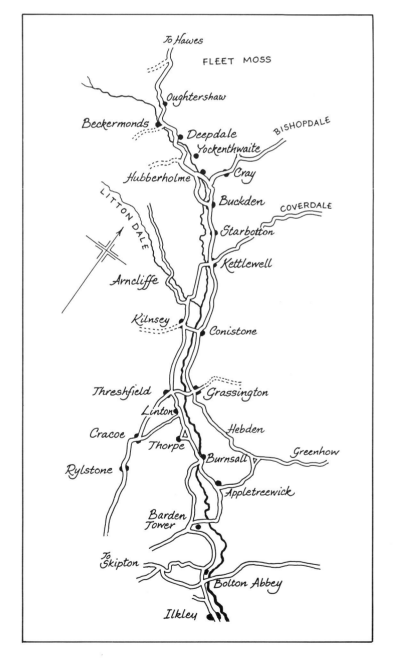

From thence commeth he to Llekeley, which considering the site in respect of *Yorke* out of *Ptolomee*, and of the affinity of the name together, I would judge to be OLICANA. Surely that is an old Towne (beside the Columnes engraven with Roman worke lying in the Churchyard and elsewhere) and was in Severus time reedified by the meanes of *Virius Lupus*, Lieutenant Generall and Propraetor then of Britaine, this inscription lately digged up hard by the Church doth plainly show:

IM. SEVERUS AUG. ET ANTONINUS CAES. DESTINATUS RESTITUERUNT CURANTE VIRIO LUPO LEGEORUM PR. P.R.*

That the second Cohort of *Lingones* abode heer, and Altar beareth witnesse which I saw there, upholding now the staires of an house, and having this Inscription set upon it by the Captaine of the second Cohort of the Lingones, to VERBEIA, haply the Nymph or Goddesse of Wharfe, the River runding there by, which River they called VERBEIA as I suppose out of so neere affinity of the names.

VERBIAE SACRUM CLODIUS FRONTO D PRAEF. COH. 11 LINGON †

William Camden, *Britannia*, 1590

*Emperors Severus, Augustus and Antoninus. Caesar elect. Restores under the care of Virius Lupus, their Legate. Pro Praetor.

† To Verbeia Sacred Clodius Fronto Ded. Prefect of the Cohort, Second Lingones.

Below Early visitors to Bolton Abbey
Opposite The White Doe of Rylstone – an engraving by Birket Foster for a Victorian edition of Wordsworth's poem, 1867

The White Doe visits Bolton Abbey

-full fifty years
That sumptuous Pile, with all its peers,
Too harshly hath been doomed to taste
The bitterness of wrong and waste:
Its courts are ravaged; but the tower
Is standing with a voice of power,
That ancient voice which wont to call
To mass or some high festival;
And in the shattered fabric's heart
Remaineth one protected part;
A Chapel, like a wild-bird's nest,
Closely embowered and trimly drest;
And thither young and old repair,
This Sabbath-day, for praise and prayer.

Fast the churchyard fills; – anon
Look again, and they are all gone;
The cluster round the porch, and the folk
Who sate in the shade of the Prior's Oak!
And scarcely have they disappeared
Ere the prelusive hymn is heard:
With one consent the people rejoice,
Filling the church with a lofty voice!
They sing a service which they feel:
For 'tis the sunrises now of zeal;
Of a pure faith the vernal prime
In great Eliza's golden time.

 A moment ends the fervent din,
All is hushed, without and within;
For though the priest, more tranquilly
Recites the holy liturgy,
The only voice which you can hear
Is the river murmuring near.
– When soft – the dusky trees between,
And down the path through the open green,
Where is no living thing to be seen;

And through yon gateway, where is found,
Beneath the arch with ivy bound,
Free entrance to the churchyard ground
Comes gliding in with lovely gleam,
Comes gliding in serene and slow,
Soft and silent as a dream,
A solitary Doe!
White she is as lily of June,
And beauteous as the silver moon
When out of sight the clouds are driven
And she is left alone in heaven;
Or like a ship some gentle day
In sunshine sailing far away,
A glittering ship, that hath the plain
Of ocean for her own domain.

William Wordsworth, *The White Doe of Rylstone*, 1808

The Historian's Challenge

After Rilston came into possession of the Cliffords, the same ground, with part of the fell above, was inclosed for a park, of which it still retains the name, and the name only.

At this time a white doe, say the aged people of the neighbourhood, long continued to make a weekly pilgrimage from hence over the fells to Bolton, and was constantly found in the abbey churchyard during divine service, after the close of which she returned home as regularly as the rest of the congregation.

This incident awakens the fancy. Shall we say that the soul of one of the Nortons had taken its abode in that animal, and was condemned to do penance, for his transgressions against — "the lord's deere" among their ashes? But for such a spirit the wild stag might have been a fitter vehicle. Was it not, then, some fair and injured female, whose name and history are forgotten? Had the milk-white doe performed her mysterious pilgrimage from Etterick Forest to the precincts of Dryburgh or Melrose, the elegant and ingenious editor of the "Border Minstrelsy" would have wrought a beautiful story.

T. D. Whitaker, *A History of Craven*, 1805

The picturesque surroundings of Bolton Abbey have long been a magnet for artists and photographers. They provided the ideal inspiration for the artist William Mellor (1851 - 1931), whose painting of Bolton Woods typifies his idealised landscapes of the River Wharfe *(opposite - courtesy Phillips of Leeds).* Trees in the same woods form a natural frame for a present-day photograph of the partially-ruined Priory *(Geoff Lund)*

Directions to Bolton Abbey

The ruins of Bolton Abbey stand upon a beautiful curvature of the 'Lordly Wharfe', on a level sufficiently high to protect it from floods, and low enough for every purpose of picturesque effect. As a ruin it is perhaps equal to any in the kingdom, if its only defect, the want of a tower, be excepted; and for surrounding scenery and beauty of its site it has not an equal.

To the south is the embrochure of the valley with its rich meadow lands, its woods and homesteads; to the right is the impetuous Wharfe, flowing beneath a wood of oaks, mingled with steep shelving ground and jutting grey rocks stained with many-hued lichens, and festooned with heather and ivy; woods to the left – to the north the eye is delighted with a park-like expanse, and beyond are those aged and noble groves that hang over the rocky river, as the valley gradually narrows, and farther yet are the barren and rugged heights of Simon Seat and Barden Fell, contrasting well with the fertility and luxuriant foliage beneath.

In walking from Bolton Bridge to the Abbey, to the south east will be noticed Beamsley Beacon on the edge of Blubber Fell, from which it is said that York Minster may be seen on a favourable day. On the left of the path is a large field in which tradition says that Prince Rupert encamped amidst the rising corn on his way to Marston Moor.

The guide's house is about a quarter of a mile from the Devonshire Arms. All the gates leading into the woods are kept locked, but any person not wishing to have a guide, may, upon inserting his name in a book kept for that purpose at the guide's house, be furnished with a key on any day except Sunday.

It is almost impossible to visit all the points of view and objects of interest at Bolton in one day. Several different routes may be taken, two of which shall here be pointed out.

The one from the Holme Terrace, by the Hall, the Strid, Devonshire Seat, to the Valley of Desolation. The return being by Park Gate Seat, and the footpath through the fields to the Devonshire Arms.

The other along the eastern bank of the Wharfe, Skiphouse Wheel Seat, Burlington Seat, Pembroke Seat, Lady Harriet's Seat, Cavendish Seat and Hartington Seat, to the Abbey.

William Howson, *An Illustrated Guide to the Curiosities of Craven*, 1850

Notice of former times directing visitors to Bolton Abbey. No photographs on Sundays!

With Wordsworth to Bolton Abbey

But you will turn again and again to the abbey to gaze on its walls archèd, the great empty window, the crumbling walls, over which hang rich masses of ivy, and walking slowly round you will discover the points whence the ruins appear most picturesque. And within, where elder-trees grow, and the carved tombstones of the old abbots lie on the turf, you may still see where the monks sat in the sanctuary, and where they poured the holy water. And whether from within or without, you will survey with reverent admiration. A part of the nave is used as a church for the neighbourhood, and ere I left, the country folk came from all the paths around, summoned by the pealing bell. I looked in and saw richly stained windows and old tombs.

On the rise above the abbey stands a castellated lodge, embodying the ancient gatehouse, an occasional resort of the late Duke of Devonshire, to whom the estate belonged. Of all his possessions this perhaps offered him most of beauty and tranquillity.

You may ramble at will; cross the long row of stepping stones on the opposite bank, and scramble through the wood to the top of the cliff; or roam over the meadows up and down the river, or lounge in idle enjoyment over the seats fixed under some of the trees. After strolling hither and thither, I concealed myself under the branches overhanging the stream, and sat there as in a bower, with my feet in the shallow water, the lively flashing current broad before me, and read,

From Bolton's old monastic tower
The bells ring loud with gladsome power ...

And while I read, the bell was ringing, and the people were gathering together, and anon the priest

– all tranquilly
Recites the holy liturgy,

but no White Doe of Rylstone came gliding down to pace timidly among the tombs, and make her couch on a solitary grave.

Wood engraving of Bolton Priory (*Marie Hartley*)

Walter White, *A Month in Yorkshire*, 1858

Barden Towers '97   Hannah Chesterman

In the Valley of Desolation

I did not want to rush upon the waterfalls, so I took a footpath going up the side of the hill in order to catch a glimpse of them first from there. The hill was bare of trees but covered with long thick grass. Coming down again, to where the slope shelved steeply down to the valley, I met two or three fine old oaks with beautiful twisted trunks, looking as if they had come straight out of some old Sung painting. A few of the branches were dead but the lower ones were covered with green leaves. The sight of old and young growing together pleased me and I made one or two rough sketches. Through the gaps between the trunks and the spaces between the branches I had glimpses of the waterfalls. The spring sun poured down on the hills with their white and green and brown, making them look warm and drowsy. Near at hand the mass of deep green oak leaves showed against the dark hollow background of the valley which stretched away grim and mysterious before me. The scene suggested adventure and inspiration for verses, and not by any means a sense of desolation. Climbing again a little I saw one of the falls streaming down like a sheet of thick silvery-white paper. The thought of it having rolled down like that for centuries made me marvel at Nature's persistence and imperturbability.

At length I began to take my way down the valley, following a narrow path which led me zig-zagging along the hillside. The sound of the falls grew louder and nearer. The woods on either side of the valley, with the hills rising behind them, seemed like the two arms of Nature spread out to enfold me. Sitting on a small rock in front of the waterfalls I felt caressed, as content and peaceful as a child in its mother's arms. Drawing a long breath I relaxed my body and smiled happily to myself. Everything was still except the cool refreshing waterfalls. There was no movement among the trees, rocks, and hills, and I felt that I must be still too. Yet the great moving mass of water seemed to fit naturally into the scene, for the more I watched it the more I had the impression that it was not moving at all. The water in the basin at the foot whirled and eddied and then flowed out into the seemingly endless valley, with the dark woods rising on either side of its silver path. I could see no living thing except one or two birds flitting among the branches of near-by trees.

Chiang Yee, *The Silent Traveller in the Yorkshire Dales*, 1940

Opposite   Barden Tower *(top)* and Simon's Seat painted by Wharfedale artist Hannah Chesterman
Right Chiang Yee's **The Silent Traveller in the Yorkshire Dales** is one of the most extraordinary books ever published on the region. The author constantly laments how the Dales remind him of home in China - a fact self-evident in his illustration of the Valley of Desolation's waterfalls

The Boy of Egremond

"Say, what remains when Hope is fled?"
She answered, "Endless weeping."
For in the herdsman's eye she read
Who in his shroud lay sleeping.

At Embsay rang the matin-bell
The stag was roused on Barden-fell;
The mingled sounds were swelling, dying,
And down the Wharfe a heron was flying;
When near the cabin in the wood
In tartan clad and forest green,
With hand in leash and hawk in hood
The Boy of Egremond was seen.
Blithe was his song, a song of yore;
But where the rock is rent in two
And the river rushes through
His voice was heard no more!
'Twas but a step! the gulf he passed;
But that step—it was his last!
As through the mist he winged his way
(A cloud that hovers night and day)

The hound hung back, and back he drew
The Master and his merlin too.
That narrow place of noise and strife
Received their little all of life!
There now the matin-bell is rung
The – "Misere!" duly sung;
And holy men in cowl and hood
Are wandering up and down the wood
But what avail they? Ruthless Lord,
Thou didst not shudder when the sword
Here on the young its fury spent,
The helpless and the innocent.
Sit now and answer groan for groan
The child before thee is thy own.
And she who wildly wanders there,
The mother in her long despair
Shall oft remind thee, waking, sleeping,
Of those who by the Wharfe were weeping;
Of those who would not be consoled
When red with blood the river rolled.

Samuel Rogers, 1819

The Terrors of the Strid

A little higher up the stream we reach the tremendous Strid; a narrow chasm in the rocks, through which the river rushes with great fury. This chasm being incapable of receiving the winter floods, has formed on either side a broad strand of native gritsone, full of rock basins, or "pots of the lin", which bear witness to the restless impetuosity of many northern torrents. The deep and solemn roar of the waters rushing through this narrow passage is heard above and beneath, amid the silence of the surrounding woods. The river boils and foams, raging and roaring like the angry spirit of the waters, in the narrow cleft of the rock, through which the current rushes with awful rapidity.

Here it was that the boy of Egremond, ranging through the woods of Barden with his hounds and huntsmen, attempted to stride across the gulph, a dangerous step:

He sprang in glee, for what cared he
That the river was strong and the rocks were steep
But the greyhound on the leash hung back
And check'd him in his leap.

The boy is in the arms of Wharf,
And strangled by a merciless force;
For never more was young Romilee seen,
Till he rose a lifeless corpse!*

The fate of the boy of Egremond has not prevented the practice of striding from bank to bank, regardless of the consequences that await a false step. The width is only four feet five inches, but few can look down into that awful gulph without a shudder of horror.

William Grainge, *The Castles and Abbeys of Yorkshire*, 1855
*Wordsworth, *Force of Prayer*.

Visitors were already flocking to The Strid when this postcard was produced in the early years of the 20th century. Some of the ladies seem dangerously close to the edge!
(Ben McKenzie collection)

At Hartlington

HALLIWELL SUTCLIFFE (1870-1932) *must undoubtedly be described as the high priest of the sentimental school of Dales topographers. Immensely popular, he was equally successful as a writer of romantic fiction – novels with such titles as* The Gay Hazard, Pam the Fiddler *and* The White Horses.
The Striding Dales, *heavy in legend and nostalgia, is still read and enjoyed with great affection throughout the former West Riding.*

You take a hill or two, and a dip, and find yourself at Hartlington, where the little bridge goes over Dibble River. It is another haunted corner of the Dale – haunted by a most exquisite and melodious peace. The hollow lies so deeply sheltered that it has a climate of its own, and in February you may find stray flowers in bloom that have not dared to bud as yet outside these charmed boundaries. The wheel of the old water-mill above is humming a cheery roundelay. The stream, brown and swift, has its own song as it swings under the grey arch; and the words of the song are yours, if you have traced it from its course on the lean highlands.

Not far above, Dibble River is no more than a beck, scolding its way between dour stones and boulders. Then its banks grow steeper and more wooded, till part of its growing flood goes by a ferny way of its own to the little lake that feeds the mill-wheel. No words can explain the beauty of that lake, its lush abandonment to all that sheltered warmth can do. The trees, wide-branched and silent, gaze at themselves in a mirror starred with waterflowers. One waits, somehow, breathless and expectant, for Elaine's barge of death to steal over the hushed waters. One almost hears Lancelot and Guinevere the Queen whispering together in the woodland, and feels Merlin's spirit brooding in the sunlit air. It is as if Lyonesse and the soft West Country had sent its heart for a sojourn in our rough and forthright highlands. Yet the stream's other part, separated at the ferny way, goes down into a gorge of wildness and of tumult. Its floods have bared gaunt roots of trees, and the flotsam lies piled in heedless disarray among the cliffs. Here at the quiet bridge the divided currents mingle and are one again; and the song of Dibble Water is all made up of parting and lone adventures and gladness in reunion.

Halliwell Sutcliffe, *The Striding Dales*, 1930

Grass Wood : Romano-British Settlement

Ageing woodland, like an old man's thinning hair
clings to the hillside, letting low shrubs twine
and riot over limestone. October brittles leaves,
hardens berries wax-bright in the still air.

Mid way in the wood a shady gorge falls
steeply east – I thought of those stubborn few
who fled to this fastness to refuse
gifts, welcome as the lash, of Latin rule.

And earlier Guevaras, nagged the famed
Imperial Legions with stray stones,
skirmishes on moonless nights, men who melted
into mysterious hills. Caesars blasphemed.

Below, the shimmering Wharfe smoothes to cities as
roads, once Roman, now bring the camera crowd,
chatter and aimless light. Farms empty.
Only the brooding ghylls dare whisper betrayals.

Colin Speakman

Above (top) Upper Wharfedale between Kilnsey Crag and Kettlewell, clearly displaying its glacial origins *(Simon Warner)*

Above (bottom) Remote Wharfedale. Waterfall in Gate Up Gill, in the middle of nowhere beyond Grimwith *(David Joy)*

Opposite Grass Wood, looking down-dale with Grassington and Simon's Seat in the distance *(Geoff Lund)*

The Awfulness of Dib Scar

After plunging again into the thicket, and pursuing the different windings which opened a passage through the wood, we were at length brought into a deep and solitary glen, beset on each side with steep and craggy precipices, whose perilous ascent made me quake as I thought of the danger I had been in had I come alone in quest of this object of nature's gloomiest contrivance. As we advanced up the avenue, the stroke of the woodman's hatchet, whom we had left on the height, which the loneliness of the place made audible, was a relief from the indescribable tremor which pervaded the senses of my guide and me, as we walked along in moody silence, making the place re-echo with the sound of our feet, which occasionally struck against some broken fragments of stones, which strewed the pathway before us. The hoarse croaking of the raven, which seemed terrified at the approach of a human footstep, and the sudden fluttering of their wings as the feathered tenantry began to forsake their lonely residence, were a signal for us to expect a speedy sight of the bluff battlement which rose on the extremities of the two environing crags. On reaching the scar we were struck with the dismalness of its appearance: its whole contour is but an expression of hoary grandeur and fallen pomp, which nothing but its hereditary strength and unbending haughtiness could have supported through so many ages. We, as it were, however, felt the power of its native dignity, and were awed in the presence of so august a monument of true and natural greatness. It forms like a huge battery on either side, and in front it resembles an old castle, built after the fashion of ancient times, with a porthole at the top, to pour unseen and immediate destruction upon an enemy, should he dare to make an encroachment on its warlike territory. The roof from off this part has been scathed, as if in some desperate struggle to maintain its hard contested right, and the batteries on either side have been partly demolished by the slow but sure engines of consuming time, but still retain their natural prowess and unshrinking attitude of self preservation, and an earthquake alone could remove them from their firm and entire foundations. The altitude of the rock, as nearly as I can guess (only judging from memory) may be about two hundred feet. The strata are irregularly placed, and beneath is a spacious canopy, perhaps seven yards high, from the base sloping upwards, under which are rows of shelves inartificially arranged, on which the weary *pilgrim* in this desolate spot may sit, and fancy himself shut up in total seclusion, so calm and peaceable is this retired haunt, so seldom visited by men.

Rev. James Leslie Armstrong, *Scenes in Craven*, in a Series of Letters containing interesting sketches of characters and notices of some of the Principal natural curiosities of the most picturesque and romantic district in Yorkshire, 1835

The Coming of the Newspapers

The deep fork of Amerdale – how descriptive ! The present name of the vale is Littondale (derived from Litton a village above Arncliffe), and its scenery is noted for being most rural and picturesque. Our notice is attracted again and again by streams of water which rush wildly into the river, their courses being a succession of beautiful cascades, whose merry voices banish for ever silence from the vale. We are now in sight of Hawkswick, and see that is is composed chiefly of respectable farmsteads; a road branches to it from the one we are in, and crosses the river by a single-arch bridge.

Owing to the village being so near Arncliffe, it can boast of neither church nor chapel, but the Wesleyans hold services there in a cottage. After walking, up hill and down, for a short distance, we reach Arncliffe, which is situated in the centre of the valley; it was at one time called "Erncleve" from a cliff that overlooks it, and which was formerly the resort of eagles. Some entymologists think the name is derived from "Tarn Cliff" and that, where the village now stands, there was once a tarn........Arncliffe also has a Cotton Mill, the machinery of which is turned by water. One thing that we soon find out about this place is the difference between its dialect and that of the greater portion of Wharfedale; the inhabitants say "noo" and "thoo" like the people of Swaledale. Another thing that we notice is the healthy, robust look of the inhabitants; and the homely and cheerful way in which they do everything cannot fail to please us. I must also tell you that the Arncliffe of today is very superior to the Arncliffe of the past, in all its features; spiritually, morally, intellectually and socially it has risen in the scale.

It has also increased its advantages; there was a time when the people knew very little of the doings of the big world; the postal arrangements were such that letters did not arrive till late in the evening, and a newspaper was one of the rarest things the villagers had the privilege to see; but, now, through improved facilities, there are few remote places in our land that are earlier supplied with information; the newspaper is no longer a stranger, and the *Craven Pioneer*, the nearest local paper, is read by the inhabitants with avidity. But we will now visit the Eagle Rock, which is a perpendicular limestone cliff, the summit of which is reached by a rugged, winding path; it is said that along its dangerous edge a person once rode after the hounds with his horse at a gallop, an adventure upon which I will leave you to make your own comments. After a toilsome ascent we are soon on the rock, some sheep which are cropping the scanty herbage, trotting away at our approach. Sit down, and look at the beauties which strike the eye....

Bailey J Harker, *Rambles In Upper Wharfedale* 1869.

Above Darnbrook, between Arncliffe and Malham. An engraving from Wordsworth's *The White Doe of Rylstone* - the poet wrote of a cottage 'hidden in the deep fork of Amerdale ... by lurking Darnbrook's pathless side'
Opposite Apart from the presence of tarmac and motor cars, Arncliffe has changed little since the publication of this early picture postcard. Bailey Harker noted that there was a time when the inhabitants 'knew very little of the doings of the big world'
(Ben McKenzie collection)

Raisgill from above Yockenthwaite, Langstrothdale (*Jacquie Denby*)

A Traveller in Mid-Victorian Times

Kettlewell (Inn: Marshall's) is a small market town inhabited largely by lead miners, and altogether a primitive little settlement. It is a place of some local importance, has three fairs a year, and gives its name to this portion of the valley of the Wharfe. The river, in its descent from the source to this point falls a depth of about 600 feet! There was formerly a small Norman church in this parish; the present is a modern one, containing however, a relic of the old edifice in a curious cylindrical Norman font. Near Kettlewell are Dove Cove and Douk Cave – the latter

is worth a visit. From Kettlewell may be made the ascent of two great mountains: one "the weather-beaten Whernside, at whose foot it stands; the best time for which is in August when the heather is in bloom and the grouse are on the wing"; the other Buckden Pike. There is a road through the pass between these heights which leads through Coverdale to Middleham in Wensleydale.

Still ascending the valley, passing Starbotton, we come to Buckden (Inns: Cock, and Buck) which is the terminus of the Wharfedale omnibus which daily conveys the "royal

The George Inn, Hubberholme - a painting by Ashley Jackson. J.B. Priestley regarded this hamlet at the head of the dale as his 'favourite place in the world' - his ashes are scattered in the churchyard

mail" from Skipton, and daily performs the return journey down the dale. From this point a road leads northwards by Bishopdale into Wensleydale, which is touched at Aysgarth – a large village four miles from Bainbridge. Buckden is a sheltered nook at the angle here formed by the course of the Wharfe; there are some good houses in the neighbourhood. The beauty of the country has been improved by recent plantations of fir trees, for which thanks must be rendered to the Hon. Mrs Ramsden. Above Buckden the valley of the Wharfe is termed Langstrothdale, usually pronounced Langsterdale. Ascending the dale, the traveller first reaches Hubberholme, where is a church with very ancient portions, and a rood-loft dated 1558 – the year of Queen Mary's death. The church was restored in 1863. Langstrothdale is believed to be the "toun" that "hight

Strother, ffer in the north," whence came the Cambridge scholars of whom we read in Chaucer's Reve's Tale. The story is considered to abound in samples of the dialect peculiar to this part of Craven. Above Hubberholme is Raisgill, and above this, Yockenthwaite; and then successfully Deepdale and Beckermonds, at the confluence of Oughtershaw Beck and Greenfield Beck.

The remotest hamlet is Oughtershaw, near which, on the slope of Cam Fell is the source of the river Wharfe. On these moors abound the scarlet cloud-berries, or nout-berries – berries larger than raspberries, but of a sickly taste, which are used by the people for tarts and puddings.

J Radford Thomson, *Guide to the District of Craven and the Settle-Carlisle Railway* 1880

Airedale and Malhamdale

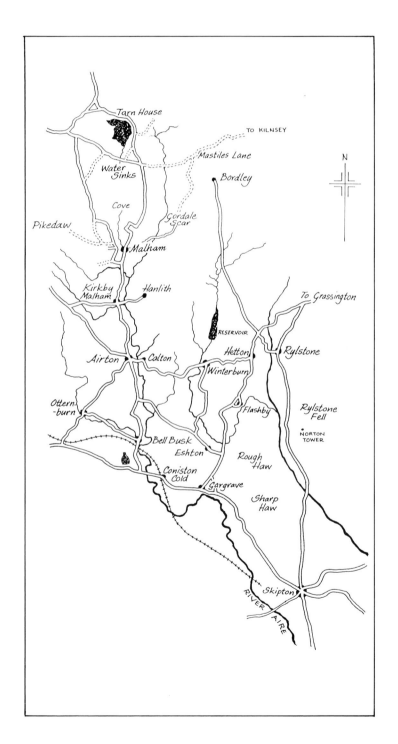

This river *Are* springing out of the hill Pennigent, which among the Westerne hils mounteth aloft above the rest, doth forthwith so sport himself with winding in an out, and doubtfull whether he should returne backe to his springhead, or runne on still to the sea, that myselfe in going directly forward on my way was faine to pass over it seven times in an houres riding. It is so calme, and milde, and carryeth so gentle ans slow a streame, that it seemeth not to runne at all but to stand still, whence I suppose it tooke the name. For, as I have said before, *Are* in the British tongue betokeneth *Milde, Still* and *Slowe*; whereupon that slow River in France *Araris* hath his name. The Country lying about the head of this River, is called in our tongue *Craven*, perchance of the British word *Crage*, that is, *a Stone*. For, the whole *Tract* there, is rough all over and unpleasant to see to, with craggy stones, hanging rocks and rugged waies; in the middest whereof, as it were in a lurking hole, not farre from *Are* standeth Skipton; and lyeth hidden and enclosed among steep Hilles, in the like manner as *Latium* in Italie, which *Varro* supposeth to have been called, because it lyeth close under the *Apennine* and the *Alps*. The Towne (for the manner of their building among these Hilles) is faire enough, and hath a very proper and strong Castle, which *Robert de Rumely* built, by whose posterity it came by inheritance to the Earles of *Aumerle*. And when their inheritance for default of heires fell by escheat into the King's hands, *Robert de Clifford*, whose heires are now Earles of Cumberland, by way of exchange obtained of King Edward the Second both this Castle, and also faire lands round about it every way, delivering into the King's hand in lieu of the same, the possessions that he had in the Marches of Wales.

William Camden, *Britannia*, 1590
translated from the Latin by Philemon Holland, 1610

The incomparable limestone scenery of Malhamdale as viewed from the top of Malham Cove *(Geoffrey N. Wright)*

At Malham Cove

In Malham Cove the stones of the brook were softer with moss than any silken pillow; the crowded oxalis-leaves yielded to the pressure of the hand, and were not felt; the cloven leaves of the herb-robert and robed clusters of its companion overflowed every rent in the rude crags with living balm; there was scarcely a place left by the tenderness of happy things where one might not lay down one's forehead on their warm softness and sleep.

John Ruskin, *Proserpina*

The State of the Roads

We now proceeded from Malham to Settle, seven miles. The road (when it can be called such) leads us over a wild, hilly country, and extensive tracts of moors. Ascending a steep hill from Malham, we come upon a rocky common, and presently lose almost every vestige of a path. Here are several pits from which calamine (a kind of fossil bituminous earth) is dug, close to the road. We continue to traverse a high, elevated country, till at length we descend rapidly to Settle, in the vale of the Ribble.

Excepting the moors, we see little besides large grazing farms, with stone walls dividing the fields. It is wholly a limestone soil, the rocks of which are peeping up above the surface very frequently, and in some places being up on the sides of the hills in awful precipices. The road is nowhere good, and some of it almost impassible, notwithstanding the abundance of excellent materials everywhere at hand: but its being not much frequented is probably the reason that so little labour and care are bestowed upon it. On the moor the traveller has no other guide than some distant mountain to direct his steps, of which he is deprived in misty weather, which is frequent in this country. When we crossed this mountainous pass, a thick mist surrounded us in darkness, and would certainly have caused us to deviate from the right path, had not the tracks of a cart, which had passed that morning from Settle to the fair at Malham, acted as a guide, and conducted us safely. This road between Settle and Malham is by no means to be recommended to strangers except in clear weather; and even then with every necessary direction and precaution; that by way of Long Preston, though tolerably good, is a circuitous route of about fifteen miles.

John Housman, *A Descriptive Tour and Guide to the Lakes Caves and Mountains and other Natural Curiosities in Cumberland, Westmorland, Lancashire and part of the West Riding of Yorkshire*, 1800 third edition, 1808

Above Bird's-eye view of Gordale Scar *(Geoff Lund)*
Opposite The old road from Malham village to the former common fields of Malham West *(Marie Hartley)*

The Horror of Gordale Scar

As I advanced the crags seem'd to close in but discovered a narrow entrance turning to the left between them. I followed my guide a few paces and lo the hills open'd again into no large space and then all further away is bar'd by a stream, that at the height of 50 feet gushes from a hole in the rock and spreading in large sheets over its broken front dashes from steep to steep and then rattles away in a torrent in the valley. The rock on the left rises perpendicular with stubbed yew trees and the shrubs, starting from its base to a height of at least 300 feet. But these are not the thing! It is that to the right and under which you stand to see these fall, that forms the principal horror of the place. From its very base it begins to slope forwards over you in one black and solid mass without any crevice in its surface and overshadows half the area below with its dreadful canopy where I stand....

. . . the gloomy and uncomfortable day well suited the savage aspect of the place and made it still more formidable. I stay'd there (not without shuddering) a quarter of an hour and thought my trouble richly paid, for the impression will last for life.

Thomas Gray, *Journal to Lord Wharton*, 11th October, 1769

The Soul of Salvator Rosa at Gordale

EDWARD DAYES (1763-1804) *was a gifted water-colourist and engraver, draughtsman of the Duke of York and an important influence on many of the younger painters of the period, particularly his own brilliant pupil Thomas Girtin and on the young Turner. His* Picturesque Tour of Yorkshire and Derbyshire *was destined to include a number of engravings, only some of which were completed, to illustrate the sublime descriptions of the text. He never lived to complete the project, dying, tragically, by his own hand in 1804. The book was published by his friends to raise money for his widow.*

Here a stupendous mass of rocks forms a ravine, through the bosom of which flows a considerable stream. This opening contracts till you are led into a corner, where every object conspires to produce one of the grandest spectacles in nature. The rocks dart their bold and rugged fronts to the heavens, and impending fearfully over the head of the spectator, seem to threaten his immediate destruction. Here rock is piled on rock in the most terrific majesty; and what greatly improves the grandeur of the scene, is an impetuous Cataract, that rushes down their dark centre, almost tearing it up, as it were, with its irresistible force, the very foundations of the earth. Good heavens, what a scene! how sublime! Imagine blocks of limestone rising to the immense height of two hundred yards, and in some places projecting twenty over their bases; add to this the roaring of the Cataract, and the sullen murmurs of the wind that howls around; and something like an idea of the savage aspect of the place may be conceived.

Here the timid will find an end put to their journey: myself and the guide, with some difficulty, ascended the crags up to the fall, keeping the water to the right hand, and arriving at a large opening, where massy fragments of rocks are scattered about in the most wild and fantastic manner. Above, through a large hole, at the height of twenty or thirty yards, poured down the collected force of the whole stream, which forms the cascade below. This is, perhaps, the finest part of the whole place, and should by no means be neglected, however difficult the ascent to it may be. Return hence was impossible; we therefore scrambled to the top of the rocks, a height of not less than three hundred yards from the stream below: here, on looking back into the yawning gulph we had passed, the words of Shakespeare came forcibly into my mind:

"Stand still - how fearful
And dizzy 'tis to cast one's eye down so low
I'll look no more,
Lest my brain turn, and the deficient sight
Topple down headlong."

The opening in the rocks, which gives passage to the stream, is said to have been carved by the force of a great body of water, which collected in a sudden storm, some time about the year 1730. The lover of drawing will be much delighted with this place: immensity and horror are its inseparable companions, uniting together to form subjects of the most awful cast. The very soul of Salvator Rosa would hover with delight over these regions of confusion.

Edward Dayes, *A Picturesque Tour in Yorkshire and Derbyshire*, 1805

Gordale's Promiscuous Ruin

My first excursion was to the *tarn* (or little lake) skirted on one side by a peat bog, and rough limestone rocks on the other; it abounds in fine trout, but has little else remarkable, except being the head of the river Air, which issuing from it, sinks into the ground very near the lake, and appears again under the fine rock which faces the village. In the time of great rains, this subterranean passage is too narrow; the brook then makes its way over the top of the rock, falling in a most majestic cascade full 60 yards in one sheet.

This beautiful rock is like the age-tinted wall of a prodigious castle; the stone is very white, and from the ledges hang various shrubs and vegetables, which with the tints given it by the bog water &c. gives it a variety that I never before saw so pleasing in plain rock.

Gordale-scar was the object of this excursion. My guide brought me to a fine sheet cascade in a glen about half a mile below the scar, the rocks of beautiful variegation and romantic shubbery. We there proceeded up the brook, the pebbles of which I found incrusted with a soft petrified coating, calcarious, slimy, and of a light brown colour.

I saw the various strata of the limestone mountains approach daylight in extensive and striking bands, running nearly horizontal, and a rent in them (from whence the brook issued) of perpendicular immense rocks.
On turning the corner of one of these, and seeing the rent in the complete – good heavens! what was my

When early tourists came to Malhamdale in the 18th century, they could still occasionally see floodwaters falling some 300 feet over the sheer face of the Cove. In more recent times the feeder streams have been swallowed by the limestone strata, depriving visitors of the stirring spectacle depicted in this engraving

astonishment! The *Alps*, the *Pyrenees, Killarney, Loch Lomond*, or any other wonder of the kind I had ever seen, do not afford such a chasm. Consider yourself in a winding street, with houses above 100 yards high on each side of you;-then figure to yourself a cascade rushing from an upper window, and tumbling over carts, waggons, fallen houses, & c. in promiscuous ruin, and perhaps a cockney idea may be formed of this tremendous cliff. But if you would conceive it properly, depend upon neither pen nor pencil, for 'tis impossible for either to give you an adequate idea of it. – I can say no more than I believe the rocks to be above 100 yards high, that in several places they project above 100 yards over the base, and approach the opposite rock so near that one would almost imagine it possible to lay a plank from one to the other. At the upper end of this rent (which may be about 300 yards horizontally long) there gushes a most threatening cascade through a rude arch of monstrous rocks, and tumbling through many fantastic masses of its own forming, comes to a rock of entire petrifaction, down which it has a variety of picturesque breaks, before it enters a channel that conveys it pretty uniformly away.

I take these whimsical shapes to be the children of the spray, formed in droughty weather, when the water has time to evaporate, and leave the stony matter uninterrupted in its cohesion. These petrifactions are very porous; crumbly when dry, and pulpy when wet, and shaped a good deal like crooked knotty wood.

Adam Walker, 20th September, 1779
Addendum to the fourth edition of West's *Guide to the Lakes*, 1789

Gordale Scar, painted by James Ward in 1811 for Lord Ribblesdale. One of the most spectacular works in the Tate Gallery, the original is no less than 14ft long by 11ft high. Ward, a quarrelsome megalomaniac, was hailed as the greatest animal painter of his day. The profusion of wild animals in the picture, many of them quite alien to the setting, exaggerate the vastness of the Scar and symbolise its savagery *(The Tate Gallery, London)*

Vendale

CHARLES KINGSLEY (1819-75), *novelist and social reformer, has achieved lasting fame with* The Water Babies. *A friend of Walter Morrison of Malham Tarn House, where he often stayed, Kingsley used the scenery of Malhamdale and Littondale (the Vendale of the novel) as the idyllic rural setting in which Tom, the pathetic child chimney-sweep can escape the cruelty and oppression of industrialism.*

A mile off, and a thousand feet down. So Tom found it; though it seemed as if he could have chucked a pebble on to the back of the woman in the red petticoat who was weeding in the garden, or even across the dale to the rocks beyond.

For the bottom of the valley was just one field broad, and on the other side ran the stream; and above it, grey crag, grey down, grey stair, grey moor, walled up to heaven.

A quiet, silent, rich, happy place; a narrow crack cut deep into the earth; so deep, and so out of the way, that the bad bogies can hardly find it out. The name of the place is Vendale; and if you want to see it for yourself, you must go up into the High Craven, and search from Bolland Forest north of Ingleborough, to the Nine Standards and Cross Fell; and if you have not found it, you must turn south, and search the Lake Mountains, down to Scaw Fell and the sea; and then if you have not found it, you must go northwards again by merry Carlisle, and search the Cheviots all across, from Annan Water to Berwick Law; and then, whether you have found Vendale or not you will have found such a country, and such a people, as ought to make you proud of being a British boy.

So Tom went to go down; and first he went down three hundred feet of steep heather, mixed up with loose brown gritstone, as rough as a file; which was not pleasant to his poor little heels, as he came bump, stump, jump, down the steep. And still he thought he could throw a stone into the garden.

Then he went down three hundred feet of limestone terraces, one below the other, as straight as if a carpenter had ruled them with his ruler and then cut out with his chisel. There was no heath there but –

First, a little grass slope, covered with the prettiest flowers, rockrose and saxifrage, and thyme and basil, and all sorts of sweet herbs.

Then bump down a two-foot step of limestone.

Then another bit of grass and flowers.

Then bump down a one foot step.

Then another bit of grass and flowers for fifty yards, as steep as the house-roof, where he had to slide down on his dear little tail.

Then another step of stone, ten feet high; and there he had to stop himself and crawl along the edge to find a crack; for if he had rolled over, he would have rolled right into the old woman's garden and frightened her out of her wits.

Then, when he had found a dark narrow crack, full of greenstalked fern, such as hangs in the basket in the drawing room, and he had crawled through it, with knees and elbows, as he would down a chimney, there was another grass slope, and another step, and so on, till – oh dear me! I wish it was all over; and so did he. And yet he thought he could throw a stone into the old woman's garden.

At last he came to a bank of beautiful shrubs; whitebeam with its great silver-backed leaves, and mountain-ash, and oak; and below them cliff and crag, cliff and crag; while through the shrubs he could see the stream sparkling, and hear it murmur on the white pebbles. He did not know it was three hundred feet below.

Charles Kingsley, *The Water Babies*, 1863

Bridge End at Arncliffe, one of the houses where Charles Kingsley stayed whilst writing The Water Babies

A Favourite View in the World

We drove home over the tops, a winding 6 mile drive of unutterable loveliness, up on to the Wuthering Heights-like expanses of Kirkby Fell, with boundless views of northern glory, and then began the descent into the serene, cupped majesty of Malhamdale, the little lost world that had been my home for seven years. Halfway down, I had my wife stop the car by a field gate. My favourite view in the world is there, and I got out to have a look. You can see almost the whole of Malhamdale; sheltered and snug beneath steep, imposing hills, with its arrow straight drystone walls climbing up impossibly ambitious slopes, its clustered hamlets, its wonderful little two-roomed schoolhouse, the old church with its sycamore and tumbling tombstones, the roof of my local pub, and, in the centre of it all, obscured by trees, our old stone house, which itself is far older than my native land.

Bill Bryson, *Notes from a Small Island* 1995

Above Drystone walls in gleaming white limestone, criss-crossing the fields at Malham
Opposite Malham Tarn, another favourite haunt of Charles Kingsley *(Simon Warner - 2)*

Ribblesdale
and the Three Peaks

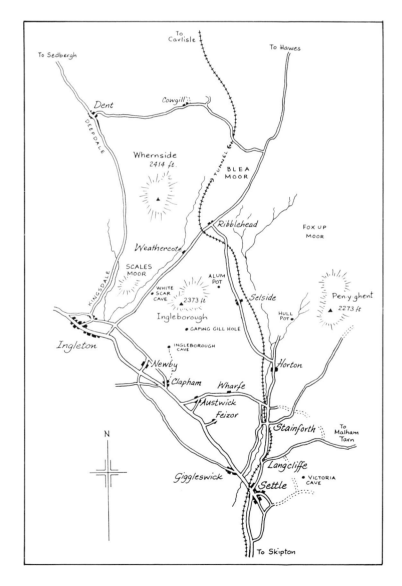

In all my spacious tract let them (so wise) survey
My Ribble's rising banks, their worst, and let them say;
At Giggleswick, where I a fountain can you show,
That eight times in a day is said to ebb and flow!
Who sometimes was a nymph, and in the mountains high
Of Craven, whose blue heads, for caps, put on the sky,
Amongst the oreads there, and sylvans, made abode
(It was ere human foot upon those hills had trod),
Of all the mountain-kind and since she was most fair;
It was a satyr's chance to see her silver hair
Flow loosely at her back, as up a cliff she clame,
Her beauties noting well, her features, and her frame,
And after her she goes; which when she did espy,
Before him, like the wind the nimble nymph did fly.
They hurry down the rocks, o'er hill and dale they drive,
To take her he doth strain, t'outstrip him she doth strive,
Like one his kind that knew, and greatly fear'd his rape,
And to the Topic gods by praying to escape,
They turn'd her to a spring, which, as she then did pant,
When, wearied with her course, her breath grew wondrous scant,
Even as the fearful nymph than thick and short did blow,
Now made by them a spring, so doth she ebb and flow.

Michael Drayton, *Polyolbion* (Song XXVIII), 1622

Three Peaks country. Neals Ing Farm, totally dwarfed by the mountain backdrop of Penyghent *(Bertram Unne)*

A Visit to Settle

Cloud berries are found plentifully on the moors between *Malham* and *Settle*. They take their name from their lofty situation. I have seen the berries in the Highlands of Scotland served as a dessert. The *Swedes* and *Norwegians* preserve great quantities in autumn to make tarts and other confections, and esteem them as excellent antiscorbatics. The *Laplanders* bruise them and eat them in the milk of reindeer, and preserve them quite fresh till spring by burying them in the snow.

I descended an exceedingly tedious and steep road, having on the right a range of rocky hills with broken precipitous fronts. At the front of a monstrous limestone rock called *Castleberg*, that threatens destruction, lies *Settle*, a small town in a little vale, exactly resembling a shabby French town with a *place* in the middle. Numbers of coiners and filers lived about the place at this time entirely out of work; by reason of the recent salutary law respecting the weight of gold.

I dined here at the neatest and most comfortable little inn I ever was at, rendered more agreeable by the civility and attention of the landlady. This is a market town, and has a small trade in knitworsted stockings, which are made here from two to five shillings a pair. The great hill of *Penygent* is seen from hence, and is about six miles distant.

Thomas Pennant, *A Tour from Downing to Alston Moor*, 1773

Lonely mountain splendour.
Above 'Proximity' by Kitty North - a painting inspired by her love of Ingleborough
Opposite Penyghent, photographed by Geoff Lund. He describes the mountain on this particular day
as resembling a lady who has just stepped out of a bubble bath!

A Remarkable Mountain

This celebrated account by a clergyman -'PASTOR' in the Gentleman's Magazine *in 1761 is rightly cited as the moment when tourism in the Dales really began. It created wide interest and many other accounts of the strange phenomena of the Ingleborough area were soon to follow.*

It is a mountain, singularly eminent, whether you regard its height, or the immense base upon which it stands. It is near 20 miles in circumference, and has *Clapham*, a church town to the South; *Ingleton* to the west; *Chapel le Dale* to the north; and *Selside*, a small hamlet to the east; from each of which place the rise, in some parts is even and gradual; in others rugged and perpendicular. In this mountain rise considerable streams, which at length fall into the Irish Sea. The land round the bottom is fine,

fruitful pasture, interposed with many acres of limestone rocks. As you ascend the mountain, the land is more barren, and under the surface is peatmoss, in many places two or three yards deep, which the country people cut up and dry for burning, instead of coal. As the mountain rises, it becomes more rugged and perpendicular, at length so steep that it cannot be ascended without great difficulty, and in some places not at all. In many parts there are fine quarries of slate, which the neighbouring inhabitants use to cover their houses; there are also many loose stones, but no limestones; yet, near the base, no stones but limestones are else found. The loose stones near the summit the people call *greet-stone*.

The foot of the mountain abounds with springs on every side, and on the west side there is a very remarkable spring near the summit. The top is very level, but so dry and barren that it offers little grass, the rock being barely covered with earth. It is said to be about a mile in circumference, and several persons now living say that they have seen races upon it. Upon that part of the top facing *Lancaster* and the *Irish Sea*, there are still to be seen the dimensions of an house, and the remains of what the country people call a beacon, viz. a place erected with stones, three or four yards high, ascended with stone stairs; which served in old times, as old people tell us, to alarm the country, upon the approach of an enemy, a person

Scaleber Force, near Settle (an illustration from Whitaker's **History of Craven**)

being always kept there upon watch, in time of war, who was to give notice in the night, by fire, to other watchmen placed upon other mountains within view, of which there are many, particularly Whernside, Woefell, Camfell, Pennygent, and Pennhill. There are likewise discoverable a great many mountains in *Westmoreland* and *Cumberland* besides the town of *Lancaster*, from which it is distant about 20 miles. The westward sides are most steep and rocky; there is, on one part to the south, where you may ascend on horseback; but whether the work of nature, or of art, I cannot say.

A part of the said mountain jutts out to the northeast near a mile, but somewhat below the summit; this is called *Park-fell*; another part jutts out in the same manner, towards the east, and is called *Simon-fell*; there is likewise another part towards the south, called *Little Ingleborough*; the summits of all of which are lower than the mountain itself. Near the base, there are holes or chasms, called swallows, supposed to be the remains of *Noah's* deluge; they are among the limestone rocks, and are open to an incredible depth.

The springs towards the east all come together, and fall into one of these swallows, or holes, called *Allun Pott*; and after passing under the earth about a mile they burst out again, and flow into the river *Ribble*, whose head, or spring, is but a little further up the valley. The depth of this swallow, or hole, could never be ascertained; it is about 20 poles in circumference, not perfectly circular, but rather oval. In wet foggy weather, it sends out a smoak, or mist, which may be seen a considerable distance. Not far from this hole, nearly north, is another hole, which may be easily descended. In some places the roof is 4 or 5 yards high, and its width the same; in other places, not above a yard; and was it not for the run of the water, it is not to be known how far you might walk, by the help of a candle, or other light. There is likewise another hole, or chasm, a little west from the other two, which cannot be descended without difficulty. You are no soon entered than you have a subterranean passage, sometimes wide and spacious, sometimes so narrow you are obliged to make use of both hands, as well as foot, to crawl a considerable way; and as I was informed, some persons have gone several hundred yards, and might have gone much further, durst they have ventured.

'Pastor', *The Gentleman's Magazine*, March 1761

Three Sublime Peaks

But the most sublime features of this romantic district are the mountains of Ingleborough, Pennigant, and Wharnside. The perpendicular height of Ingleborough is, according to Mr. Jeffrey, exactly one mile above the level of the sea, but by other measurements and calculations it is much less. The base of this mountain is an immense mass of limestone; but towards the summit the rock is for the most part a sandy grit. The eastern and southern sides are extremely steep, the latter bending in the form of a crescent, with a deep morass at the bottom. On this side a boggy moor, and above half a mile in breadth, must be crossed in approaching the mountain from the village of Austwick, by the way of Cromack Farm, the nearest road from Settle. The north side of Ingleborough is less steep than the eastern and southern sides; but the western side is the most sloping, and the easiest ascent from eastern and southern sides. (The writer thinks it not amiss to mention this circumstance, and would advise every tourist that visits Ingleborough, or other mountains of this district, to provide himself with a guide; for want of this precaution he found himself bewildered amidst the rocks and morasses, and found the approach to Ingleborough on the southern side, from the village of Austwick, very laborious, chiefly through ignorance of the road.)

The sides, where not perpendicular, are springy: the ground indeed, to the very summit, emits water at every pore; for this mountain being the first check that the western clouds meet with in their passage from Ireland, is almost continually enveloped in mists, or washed with rains, which occasion an extraordinary degree of humidity. From this cause, however, the soil is covered with verdure, and flocks of sheep graze on the highest parts of the mountain. The top of Ingleborough is level and horizontal, extending in nearly an easterly and westerly direction, about half a mile in length, but of much less breadth. Here was formerly placed a beacon for giving the alarm to the country in case of sudden danger, particularly during the incursions of the Scots. From this stupendous elevation the prospects are romantic, sublime and extensive. To the east, the picturesque country of Craven presents a confused assemblage of hills, gradually diminishing in height, till they vanish in the horizon. Pennigant at the distance of four miles, appears almost within a leap. Towards the south, the rocks near Settle and Pendle hill, towering aloft seem close at hand. The northern and north-western prospect exhibits a mass of mountains; Wharnside is within distance of six miles; Snowden, Cross-fell etc. are clearly visible. Towards the west, the flat country of Lancashire lies as in a map. And the prospect extends far into the Irish sea, the nearest shores of which are almost 24 miles from Ingleborough. This mountain is said to be the first land that sailors descry in the voyage from Dublin to Lancaster. About the base are many deep holes or pits, called swallows.

Pennigant, about seven miles north from Settle, and four miles south east from Ingleborough, is a steep and towering mountain, of which the perpendicular height, according to Mr Jeffrey's measurement, is 1740 yards above the level of the sea. At its base are two frightful orifices, called Hulpit and Huntpot holes: the former looks like the ruins of a large castle, with the roof fallen in and the walls standing; the latter resembles a deep funnel. Through each of these runs a subterraneous brook, passing underground for about a mile, and then emerging, one at Dowgill-Scar, and the other at Bransil Head.

Whernside, the highest mountain in either England or Wales, is situated about six miles to the northwest of Ingleborough in the midst of a vast amphitheatre of hills. Its perpendicular height is, according to Mr Jeffrey, 5340 feet, or one mile and 20 yards above the level of the sea. Near the summit are several pools or small lakes here called tarns, two of which are at least 180 yards in length, and but little less in breadth. The prospects from the top of this mountain are very extensive, and towards the east remarkably fine, commanding the whole of the beautiful vale of Wensleydale and its neighbouring scenery; but, like those of Ingleborough, they are often obscured by the mists and clouds which so frequently envelope these elevated regions.

John Bigland, *The Beauties of England and Wales*
Volume XVI, 1812

Above One of the most famous views in the Three Peaks country. Seen from the Langcliffe to Malham Moor road, superb limestone pavement in the foreground contrasts with the hamlet of Upper Winskill in the middle distance and flat-topped Ingleborough on the skyline.

Opposite Whernside, which early travellers thought to be over a mile high and England's loftiest peak. Ribblehead viaduct on the famous Settle to Carlisle railway runs across the centre of the picture. ***(Marie Hartley - 2)***

Ribblesdale

Earth, sweet Earth, sweet landscape, with leavès throng
and louchèd low grass, heaven that does appeal
To, with no tongue to plead, no heart to feel:
That canst but only be, but dost that long -

Thou canst but be, but that though well dost: strong
Thy plea with him who dealt, nay does now deal,
Thy lovely dale down thus and thus bids reel
Thy river, and o'er gives all to rack or wrong.

And what is Earth's eye, tongue or heart else, where
Else, but in dear and dogged man ? Ah, the heir
To his own selfbent so bound, so tied to his turn,
To thriftless reave both our rich round world bare
And non reck of world after, this bids wear
Earth brows of such care, care and dear concern.

Gerard Manley Hopkins

Underground wonderland.   The Main Chamber of Gaping Gill - Britain's largest known cavern (*John & Eliza Forder*)

Weathercote Cave
- Sublime and Terrible

... we proceeded about a hundred and twenty yards higher when we came to *Weathercote-cave* or cove the most surprising natural curiosity of the kind in the island of *Great Britain*. It is a stupendous subterranean cataract in a huge cave, the top of which is on the same level with the adjoining lands. On our approach to its brink, our ears and eyes were equally astonished with the sublime and terrible. The margin was surrounded with trees and shrubs, the foliage of which was of various shapes and colours, which had an excellent effect, both in guarding and ornamenting the steep and rugged precipices on every side. Where the eye could penetrate through the leaves and branches, there was room for the imagination to conceive this cavern more dreadful and horrible, if possible, than it was in reality. The cave is of a lozenge form, and divided into two by a rugged and grotesque arch of limestone rock: The whole length from south to north is about sixty yards, and the breadth about half its length. At the south end is the entrance down into the little cave; in the right of which is a subterranean passage under the rocks, and a petrifying well: A stranger cannot but take notice of a natural seat and table in a corner of this grotesque room, well suited for a poet or philosopher: Here he may be secluded from the bustle of the world, though not from the noise; the uniform roaring however of the cascades will exclude from the ear every other sound, and his retirement will conceal him from every object that might divert the eye. Having descended with caution from rock to rock, we passed under the arch and came into the great cave, where we stood some time in silent astonishment to view this amazing cascade. The perpendicular height of the north corner of this cave, was found by an exact measurement to be thirty six yards; near eleven yards from the top issues a torrent of water out of an hole in the rock, about the dimensions of the large door in a church, sufficient to turn several mills, with a curvature which shews, that it has had a steep descent before it appears in open day; and falls twenty five yards at a single stroke on the rocks at the bottom, with a noise that amazes the most intrepid ear. The water sinks as it falls amongst the rocks and pebbles at the bottom, running by a subterranean passage about a mile, where it appears by the side of the turnpike road, visiting on its way other caverns of *Ginglepot* and *Hurtlepot*. The cave is filled with the spray that arises from the water dashing against the bottom, and the sun happening to shine very brightly, we had a small vivid rainbow within a few yards of us, for colour, size and situation, perhaps nowhere else to be equalled. An huge rock that had sometimes been rolled down by the impetuosity of the stream, and was suspended between us and the top of the cascade, like the coffin of *Mahomet* at *Medina*, had an excellent effect in the scene, Though the stream had polished the surfaces of the pebbles on which it fell at the bottom by rolling them against each other; yet its whole force was not able to drive from its native place the long black moss that firmly adhered to the large immoveable rocks. We were tempted to descend into a dark chamber at the very bottom of the cave, covered over with a ceiling of rock above thirty yards thick, and from thence behind the cascade, at the expense of having our cloaths a little wet and dirtied, when the noise became tremendous, and the idea for personal safety awful and alarming. We were informed that in a great drought the divergency of the stream is so small that we might with safety go quite round the cascade. At the bottom we were shewn a crevice where we might descend to the subterranean channel, which would lead us to *Ginglepot*, and perhaps much further; we were also shewn above, a shallow passage between the strata of rocks, along which we might crawl to the orifice out of which the cascade issued, where it was high enough to walk erect, and where we might have the honour of making the first expedition for discoveries; no creature having yet proceeded in that passage out of sight of daylight: But as we were apprehensive the pleasures would not be compensated by the dangers and difficulties in our progress, we did not attempt to explore these new regions.

John Hutton, *A Tour to the Caves*, 1781

Weathercote Cave, painted by J.M.W. Turner in 1817-18. The artist visited this 'stupendous subterranean cataract' when it was in flood and the cave entrance was half-filled with water *(British Museum)*

A Horrid Place

The first curiosity we were conducted to was *Hurtlepot*, about eighty yards above the chapel. It is a round deep hole, between thirty and forty yards in diameter surrounded with rocks almost on all sides, between thirty and forty feet perpendicular above a deep black water, in a subterranean cavity at its bottom. All round the top of this horrid place are trees, which grew secure from the axe: their branches almost meet in the centre, and spread a gloom over a chasm dreadful enough of itself without being heightened with any additional appendages: It was indeed one of the most dismal prospects I had yet been presented with. The descent of *Aeneas* into the infernal regions came fresh into my imagination....

After viewing for some time with horror and astonishment its dreadful aspect from the top, we were emboldened to the margin of this Avernian lake. What its depth is we could not learn: but from the length of time the sinking stones we threw in continued to send up bubbles from the black abyss, we concluded it to be very profound. How far it extended under the huge pendent rocks we could get no information, a subterranean embarkation having never yet been fitted out for discoveries. In great flood we were told this pot runs over; some traces of it then remained on the grass. While we

Main Stream Passage, Lancaster Hole
(John & Eliza Forder)

stood at the bottom, the awful silence was broken four or five times in a minute by drops of water falling into the lake from the rocks above, in different solemn keys. The sun shining on the surface of the water, illuminated the bottom of the superincumbent rocks, only a few feet above; which, being viewed by reflection in the lake, caused a curious deception, scarce any where to be met with: They appeared at the like distance below its surface in form of a rugged bottom. But alas! How fatal would be the consequence if any adventurer should attempt to wade across the abyss on this fallacious principle. This deep is not without its inhabitants; large black trout are frequently caught in the night by the neighbouring people.

John Hutton, *A Tour to the Caves*, 1781

The Stygian Gulphs of Ribblesdale

Horton is about six miles from Settle, and the last village on the upper road to Askrigg. From Horton I immediately entered on the moors, where all is dreary, wild and solitary. Having proceeded about a mile, I was surprised by a most horrid roaring to the right, which I discovered to arise from a considerable stream ingulphen by a chasm, as black as the entrance into the informal regions.* It is reported, but the tale is rather improbable, that a short time ago a person was let down into this gulph by a rope, to the depth of one hundred; but his courage failing him, he roared out lustily, and his companions drew him up again. I threw several large stones into this Stygian gulph but could not hear when they reached the bottom.

Scarcely had the surprise excited by the above spectacle subsided, when the road again brought me on to the edge of a precipice, where the River Ribble is dashed from rock to rock in wild variety. †Here Silence never dwells, but horrid Uproar holds his everlasting reign! This place does not prevent a single fall only, but a succession of them, where cataract tumbles over cataract; the power of the water having a passage under a solemn mass of rock, the bulk of which is incredible, and from it issues with a hideous din, that deafens the sense. In some places the water by undermining the crags, has precipitated huge fragments in the gulph below. With such a scene under the eye, alone on an open moor, the heavens foreboding a storm, and not a single habitation to be seen as far the utmost stretch of human ken, what language could be adequate to describe its effects on the mind, or the feelings it excited! A considerable quantity of rain having fallen, it contributed greatly to increase the grandeur of the whole. Those who are fond of the wild, will find enough to satisfy them: but it would be advisable to engage the attendance of some person from Horton who, by possessing a knowledge of the paths, might be able to shew them its wonder from below. My being alone, prevented me from descending into these scenes of chaotic confusion.

The road in many places runs along the edge of steep declivities, down which there is great danger of being precipitated, particularly in stormy weather. It is reported that a lady and gentleman in a postchaise, venturing this way, were blown over, and narrowly escaped falling to the bottom. Scarcely a tree is to be seen, and all the mighty expanse consists but of one tiresome sweep intersecting another.

Edward Dayes, *A Picturesque Tour in Yorkshire and Derbyshire*, 1805

*I think this place is called Hunt Pot.
†Probably called Lingill.

A Glittering Fairy Palace

WALTER WHITE (1811-93) *of Berkshire was a thoroughly professional journalist, essayist and traveller. After the break-up of his marriage in the 1840s, he spent several years travelling in Britain and Europe, producing a number of popular travel books, including the immensely popular* A Month in Yorkshire *which continued to be reprinted right until the end of the nineteenth century.*

Here in Clapdale, a dale which penetrates the slopes of Ingleborough is the famous Ingleborough Cave, the deepest and the most remarkable of all the ones hitherto discovered in the honeycombed flanks of that remarkable hill. Interested to see this, I left unvisited the other caves which have yet been mentioned as lying to the right and left of the road as you come from Gearstones.

The fee for a single person to see the cave is half-a-crown; for a party of eight in turn a shilling each. The guide, who is an old soldier, and a good specimen of his class, civil and intelligent, called at his house as we passed to get candles, and presently we were clear of the village, and walked uphill along a narrow lane. Below us on the right lay cultivated grounds and well-kept plantations, through which, as the old man told me, visitors were once allowed to walk on their way to the cave – a pleasing and much less toilsome way than the lane, but the remains of picnics left on the grass, broken bottles, greasy paper and wisps of hay, became such a serious abuse, that Mr Farrer, the proprietor, withdrew his permission. "It's a wonder to me," said the guide, "that people shouldn't know how to behave themselves."

In about half an hour we came to a hollow between two grassy acclivations, out of which runs a rapid beck, and here on the left, in a limestone cliff prettily screened by trees, is the entrance to the cave, a low, wide arch, that narrows as it reaches into the gloom. We walked in a few yards; the guide lit two candles, placed one in my hand and unlocked the iron gate which, very properly, keeps out the perpetrators of wanton mischief. A few paces takes us beyond the last gleam of daylight, and we come to a narrow passage, of which the sides and roof are covered with a brown incrustation resembling gigantic clusters of petrified moss. Curious mushroom-like growth hung from the roof, and throwing his light on them, the guide says we are passing through the Inverted Forest. So it continues, the roof still low, for eighty yards, comprising the Old Cave, which has been known for ages; and we come to a narrow passage hewn through a thick screen of stalagmite. It was opened twenty years ago by Mr Farrer's gardener, who hacked at the barrier until it was breached, and a new cavern of marvellous formation was discovered beyond. An involuntary exclamation broke from me as I entered and beheld what might have been taken for a glittering fairy palace. On each side, sloping gently upwards till they met the roof, great bulging masses of stalagmite of snowy whiteness lay outspread, mound after mound glittering as with millions of diamonds. For the convenience of explorers, the passage between them has been widened and levelled as far as possible, whilst the beck that we saw outside fills a channel after unusual rains. You walk along this passage now on sand now on pebbles, now on bare rock. All the great white masses are damp, their surfaces are rough with countless crystallised convolutions and minute ripples, between which trickle here and there tiny threads of water. It is to the moisture that the unsullied whiteness is due, and the glistening effect; for wherever stalactite or stalagmite becomes dry,

Illusion Pot, Kingsdale - one of the many 'glittering fairy palaces' which lie beneath the surface of the Dales (*H. Limbert*)

the colour changes to brown, as we saw in the Old Cave. A strange illusion came over me as I passed slowly across the undulating ranges, and for a moment they seemed to represent the great rounded snow fields that whiten the sides of the Alps.

The cave widens: we are in Pillar Hall; stalactites of all dimensions hang from the roof, singly and in groups. Thousands are mere nipples, or an inch or two in length; many are two or three feet; and the whole place echoes with the drip and tinkle of water. Stalagmites dot the floor, and while some have grown upwards the stalactites have grown downwards, until the ends meet, and the ceaseless trickle of water fashions an unbroken crystal pillar. Some stalactites assume a spiral twist; and when this first occurs in the roof they take the form of draperies, curtains and wings – many shaped like those of angels. The guide strikes one of the wings with a small mallet, a rich musical note; another has a deep sonorous boom of a cathedral bell, another rings sharp and shrill, and now a stalactite sheet answers when touched with a gamut of notes. Your imaginative powers stir whilst you listen to such strange music in the heart of a mountain.

Walter White, *A Month in Yorkshire*, 1858

Dentdale, Garsdale and the Howgills

Arrived at Dent, after a tedious and disagreeable journey, having, in the course of it, passed through a small part of Lancashire, and travelled about eight miles in the county of Westmoreland.

We enter Dent Dale from the west, and proceeded down the Dale to the town of Dent, which is nearly in the centre. This Dale is entirely surrounded with high mountains, and has only one opening in the west, where a carriage may enter with safety. It is about 12 miles in length, and from one and a half to two miles in breadth. The whole Dale is enclosed; and viewed from the higher grounds, presents a picture of a terrestrial paradise.

At Dent we received the following information relevant to the state of the Dale. Estates are small, and chiefly in the actual possessions of the proprietors. Inclosures are small; and mostly grass. No farms above £50 a year, and none but yearly leases are granted. Sheep mostly from Scotland, but a great number of milch cows are kept, and large quantities of butter and cheese produced. The hills in the neighbourhood of the Dale, are all common, and dividing them among the different proprietors, it is supposed, would be attended with beneficial consequences. A considerable quantity of stockings wrought by women upon wires, which are disposed of at Kendal. Very few turnips cultivated, hay being the chief dependence in winter.

From the Journal of the Survey made by Rennie, Brown and Sherriff, 1793
in *A General View of Agriculture of the West Riding of Yorkshire*

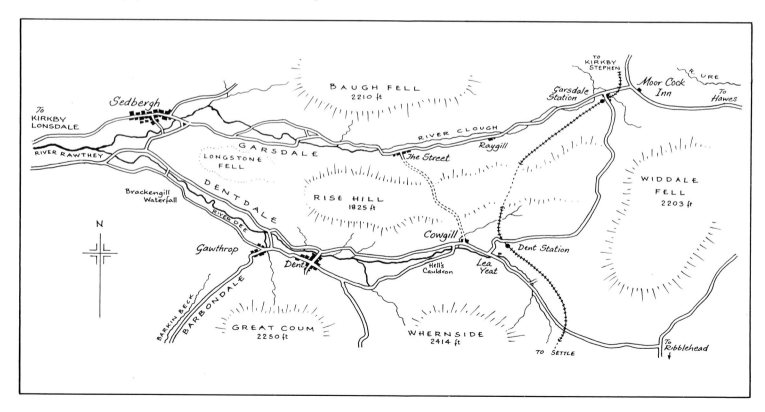

Winter morning at Dent Town - 'the bonniest of all Dales villages' *(Geoffrey N. Wright)*

No Chocolate Box Village

In my opinion the loveliest of all the dales, Dentdale is also the most secluded, cut off both by the hills which hem in eastern and western ends, and by the narrowness of the roads that lead in and out of it. At Dentdale's eastern end, Dent Head and the viaduct lead into the dale, the road winding on to Lea Yeat and Cowgill where the narrow winding Coal Road climbs by Monkeybeck Grains and below Shaking Moss over into Garsdale, its highest point often being blocked by snow in the winter months. The Dentdale road carries on from Cowgill by the chapel past Scotchergill and on by Church Bridge to Dent 'Town' as the village is called. West of Dent the road passes by Helmside and climbs the foot of Frostrow by Millthrop into the 'big city' of Sedbergh behind which looms the great Howgill Fells.It may be the fact that this end of the dale is shielded by the Howgills and the other by Wold Fell and Blea Moor, which, combined with its narrowness, makes Dentdale so lush and green – I don't know. But it does seem (and locals swear) that the climate is milder in Dentdale than the rest of the Dales. It gets less rain they say, and the snow if it does fall never lies long. It's a woody dale, with more trees than many of the other dales, and hedges replace the stone walls of the limestone country. Be that as it may Dentdale certainly is, as I have said, the bonniest of all the Dales and Dent village with its cobbled streets and whitewashed houses, the bonniest of all the Dales villages.

Dent has been called a 'chocolate-box village' by some writers who have assumed that the preservation of the village is due to the action of the green welly and Barbour jacket brigade (2.4 children called Timon and Amarintha, Range Rover with macramé or tie-die seatcovers and this year's Booker Prize winner on the back seat), but the fight to prevent the cobbles being ripped up and the narrow bridges widened was led, not by middle class 'off-comed-uns', but by Dalesfolk, the farmers, joiners and builders, the ordinary people who cared about their dale.

Mike Harding, *Walking the Dales* 1986

Spring Journey

Brag, sweet tenor bull,
descant on Rawthey's madrigal,
each pebble its part
for the fells' late spring.
Dance tiptoe, bull,
black against may.
Ridiculous and lovely
chase hurdling shadows
morning into noon.
May on the bull's hide
and through the dale
furrows fill with may,
paving the slowworm's way.

A mason times his mallet
to a lark's twitter
listening while the marble rests
lays his rule at a letter's edge
fingertips checking
till the stone spells a name,
naming none,
a man abolished.
Painful lark, labouring to rise!
The solemn mallet says:
In the grave's slot
he lies. We rot.

Decay thrusts the blade
wheat stands in excrement
trembling. Rawthey trembles.
Tongue stumbles, ears err
for fear of spring.
Rub the stone with sand,
wet sandstone rending
roughness away. Fingers
ache on the rubbing stone.

The mason says: Rocks
happen by chance.
No one here bolts the door,
love is so sore.

Stone smooth as skin
cold as the dead they load
on a low lorry by night.
The moon sits on the fell
but it will rain.
Under sacks on the stone
two children lie,
hear the horse stale,
the mason whistle,
harness mutter to the shaft
felloe to axle squeak,
rut thud the rim
crushed grit.

Stocking to stocking, jersey to jersey,
head to hard arm,
they kiss under rain,
bruised by their marble bed.
In Garsdale, dawn;
at Hawes, tea from the can.
Rain stops, sacks
steam in the sun, they sit up.
Copper-wire moustache,
sea-reflecting eyes
and Baltic plainsong speech
declare: By such rocks
men killed Bloodaxe.

Fierce blood throbs in his tongue,
lean words.
Skulls cropped for steel caps

River Dee at Harbour Gill, Dentdale *(Simon Warner)*

huddle around Stainmore.
Their becks ring on limestone,
whisper to peat.
The clogged cart pushes the horse downhill.
In such soft air

They trudge and sing,
laying the tune frankly on the air.
All sounds fall still,
fellside bleat,
hide-and-seek-peewit.

Basil Bunting, from *Briggflatts*, 1965

The Little World of
Dentdale

About mid-way in the valley lies its hamlet, called Dent-town – a Swiss-like village, embosomed in hills, with its picturesque houses, many of which have remarkable projecting roofs and outside staircases, leading, by a little gallery, into the chambers; its low-spired church or "kirk" as it is called, and its old-fashioned endowed school, of which we shall have more to say anon.

The only road in the valley follows the course of the river, excepting where that course is meandering. Like a sedate man of business and a playful child, so proceed together the road and the little river.

The homesteads of the dale lie scattered on the hill-sides, being generally erected near those water-courses, or gills, as they are called, which, proceeding from the bogs of the hill-tops, form themselves into rivulets and have worn channels down the rocky hill-sides. They are diversified by occasional abrupt and picturesque falls, and often from their highest descent are margined by trees.

The little world of Dentdale, as viewed from the summit of Winder. Sedbergh is in the foreground
(Geoffrey N. Wright)

Nothing can be more delightful than these clear little streams, hurrying down with living voices, each a willing tributary to the cheerful river.

As in the case in these dales, the good people of Dentdale form a little world in themselves. Each is generally the proprietor of his own section of the hill-side – that is between rivulet and rivulet—which form the natural landmarks of each demesne. Two or three fields, called "pastureheads" are generally enclosed and cultivated near the house, where oats, wheat, and potatoes are grown for family consumption; and the lower descent of the hill, down to the level of the valley, is used for grass and hay for the horses and cows; but the upper parts, called "the fell-side" are grazed by large flocks of sheep, geese, and wild ponies. Sheep, however, form the wealth of the valleys; and the sheepwashings and shearings make as blithe holidays as the harvest-homes, and the wakes and fairs, of other districts.

The greatest sociality exists among the inhabitants of this simple district, occasioning as much visiting as in more dignified and gayer society. In order that the Dee – for such is the name of the river – may interpose no barrier to the intercourse of the opposite sides of the valley, it is crossed by many little stone bridges and stepping-stones. In hot weather the dale children may be seen, on their return from school, dabbling in the water, with their shoes and stockings off, catching fish or hopping from stone to stone, playing a hundred vagaries, any of which would alarm a city mother.

Besides their small agricultural occupation, and the tending of their feathered and woolly flocks, the dales people have another employment, which engrosses a great portion of time; this is knitting. Old men and young, women and children, all knit. The aged man, blind and decrepit, sits on the stone seat at the door, mechanically pursuing this employment, which seems as natural to his hands as breathing to his lungs. The old woman, the parent of three generations, sits in the chimney-corner knitting, while she rocks, with her foot, the wooden cradle in which lies the youngest-born of the family. The intermediate generations have their knitting likewise, which they take up and lay down as their daily vocations allow. The little intercourse that the dales-people have with the rest of the world, makes them almost unconscious of the singularity of this employment. For aught they know to the contrary, the rest of England knit as much as they. Although a rumour of railroads, power-looms, and wove stockings has reached them, they still find a demand in Kendal for their goods; and, though everyone says the trade was better in their father's time, they still go on knitting, contented in the belief that, while the world stands, stockings and caps will be wanted; and consequently, that the dales people will always be knitters. Such is Dentdale, and such is its people.

Mary Howitt, "Dentdale Fifty Years Ago", 1840 from *Hope on! Hope Ever!*

Wensleydale

Wensleydale, a beautiful fertile vale, narrow, bounded by high hills, inclosed with hedges, and cultivated far up, in many parts cloathed with woods, surmounted by long ranges of scars, white rocks, smooth and precipitous in front, and perfectly even at their tops. The rapid crystal Ure devides the whole, fertilising the rich meadows with its stream....

Reach *Aysgarth* or Aysgarth Force, remarkable for the fine arch over the Ure built in 1539. The scenery above and below is most uncommonly picturesque. The banks on both sides are lofty, rocky, and darkened with trees. Above the bridge two regular precipices cross the river, down which the water falls in beautiful cascades, which are seen to great advantage from below. The gloom of the pendant trees, the towering steeple of the church above, and the rage of the waters beneath the ivybowered arch, form together a most romantic view ...

... The eye is finely directed to this beautiful cataract by the scars that board the river, being lofty, precipitous and quite of a smooth front, and their summits fringed with hollies and other trees....

Thomas Pennant, *Second Tour in Scotland*, 1772 (1776 edition)

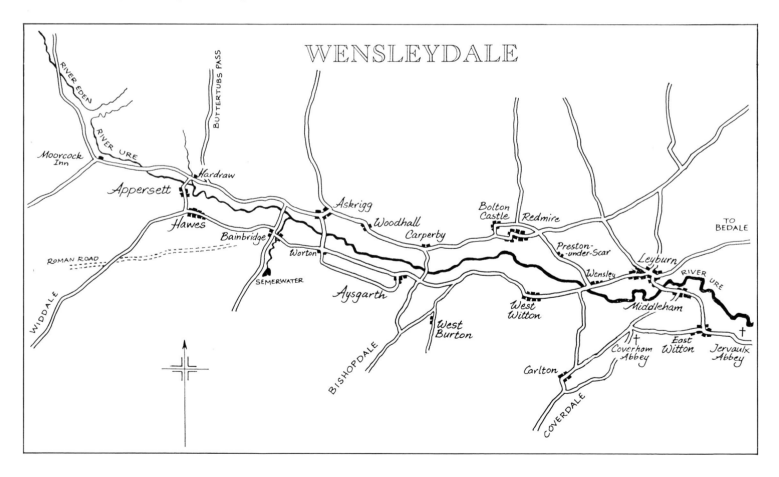

April shower in Wensleydale *(etching by Piers Browne)*

Middleham Castle

ALFRED TENNYSON *toured Wensleydale and Wharfedale during the summer of 1862 in the company of F.T. Palgrave, the poet and anthologist. He later told his son, Hallam, that Middleham Castle had partly inspired his description of Yniol's Castle in "Enid", the first of his celebrated* Idylls of the King *which at that time he was in the process of revising.*

At last they issued from the world of wood
And climb'd upon a fair and even ridge,
And show'd themselves against the sky, and sank.
And thither came Geriant, and underneath
Beheld the long street of a little town
In a long valley, on one side of which,
White from the mason's hand, a fortress rose;
And on one side a castle in decay,
Beyond a bridge that spann'd a dry ravine:
And out of town and valley came a noise
As of a broad brook o'er a shingly bed
Brawling, or like the clamour or the rooks
At distance, ere they settle for the night....
    . . . Then rode Geriant into the castle court,

His charger trampling many a prickly star
Of sprouted thistle on the broken stones.
He look'd, and saw that all was ruinous.
Here stood a shatter'd archway plumed with fern;
And here had fallen a great part of a tower,
Whole, like a crag that tumbles from the cliff,
And like a crag was gay with wilding flowers:
And high above a piece of turret stair,
Worn by the feet that now were silent, wound
Bare to the sun, and monstrous ivy-stems
Clasp the gray walls with hairy-fibred arms,
And suck'd the joining of the stones, and look'd
A knot, beneath, of snakes, aloft a grove.

Alfred Tennyson, from "Enid", *Idylls of the King*, 1863

Middleham Castle (**wood engraving by Marie Hartley**)

Hart Leap Well

HART LEAP WELL *is situated by the roadside alongside the old Askrigg-Richmond road, a short distance to the west of Catterick Camp, capped in incongruous concrete and on the edge of a military training area. Wordsworth's poem, from his early* Lyrical Ballads *period, uses the legend of the hunted deer, on the site of whose deathleap an ornamental well-head was constructed, as a fable of man's callousness against the innocence of Nature – a theme which runs through much Romantic literature.*

As I from Hawes to Richmond did repair,
It chanced that I saw standing in a dell
Three aspens at three corners of a square;
And one, not four yards distant, near a well.

What this imported I could ill divine:
And, pulling now the rein my horse to stop,
I saw three pillars standing in a line,—
The last stone-pillar on a dark hill-top.

The trees were grey, with neither arms nor head;
Half wasted the square mound of tawny green;
So that you just might say, as then I said,
Herein old time the hand of man hath been.

I looked upon the hill both far and near,
More doleful place did never eye survey;
It seemed as if the spring-time came not here,
And Nature here were willing to decay.

I stood in various thoughts and fancies lost,
When one, who was in shepherd's garb attired,
Came up to the hollow: – him did I accost,
And what this place might be I then enquired.

The Shepherd stopped, and that same story told
Which in my former rhyme I have rehearsed.
A jolly place," said he, – in times of old!
But something ails it now: the spot is curst.

"You see these lifeless stumps of aspen wood –
Some say they are beeches, others elms –
These were the bower; and here a mansion stood,
The finest palace of a hundred realms!

"The arbour does its own condition tell;
You see the stones, the fountains, and the stream;
But as to the great Lodge! you might as well
Hunt half a day for a forgotten dream.

"There's neither dog nor heifer, horse nor sheep
Will wet his lips within that cup of stone;
And oftentimes, when all are fast asleep,
This water doth send forth a dolorous groan.

"Some say that here a murder has been done,
And blood cries out for blood: but, for my part,
I've guessed, when I've been sitting in the sun,
That it was all for that unhappy Hart."

William Wordsworth, from *Hart Leap Well*, 1799

Aysgarth Falls have long captivated visitors to Wenselydale. In his 18th century journals, which have been described as 'books that are as dull as they are valuable', Bishop Pococke commented that the Falls were superior to the cataracts of the Nile! *(Simon Warner)*

The Wordsworths in Wensleydale - 1

When we passed through the village of Wensly my heart was melted away with dear recollections, the Bridge, the little water-spout, the steep hill, the Church. They are among the most vivid of my own inner visions, for they were the first objects that I saw after we were left to ourselves, and had turned our whole hearts to Grasmere as a home in which we were to rest. The Vale looked most beautiful each way. To the left the bright silver stream inlaid the flat and very green meadows, winding like a serpent. To the Right we did not see it so far, it was lost among trees and little hills. I could not help observing as we went along how much more *varied* the prospects of Wensly Dale are in summer time than I could have thought possible in the winter. This seemed to be in great measure owing to the trees being in leaf, and forming groves, and screens, and thence little openings upon recesses and concealed retreats which in winter only made part of the one great vale. The *beauty* of the summer time here as much excels that of the winter as the variety, owing to the excessive greeness of the fields, and the trees in leaf half concealing, and where they do not conceal, softening the hard bareness of the limey white roofs. One of our horses seemed to grow a little restive as we went through the first village, a long village on the side of a hill. It grew worse and worse, and at last we durst not go on any longer. We walked a while, and then the Post-Boy was obliged to take the horse out and go back for another. We seated ourselves again snugly in the Post-Chaise. The wind struggled about us and rattled the window and gave a gentle motion to our chaise, but we were warm and at our ease within. Our station was at the Top of a hill, opposite Bolton Castle, the Eure flowing beneath. William has since wrote a sonnet on this our imprisonment – Hard was the Durance Queen compared with ours. Poor Mary! Wm. fell asleep, lying upon my breast and I upon Mary. I lay motionless a long time, but I was at last obliged to move. I became very sick and continued so for some time after the Boy brought the horse to us. Mary had been a little sick but it soon went off. We had a sweet ride till we came to a public house on the side of a hill where we alighted and walked down to see the waterfalls. The sun was not yet set, and the woods and fields were spread over with the yellow light of Evening, which made their greeness a thousand times more green. There was too

Bolton Castle, as it looked in the late 18th century when painted by Thomas Girtin (*Ashmolean Museum, Oxford*)

much water in the River for the beauty of the falls, and even the banks were less interesting than in winter. Nature had entirely got the better in her struggles against the giants who first cast the mould of these works; for indeed it is a place that did not in winter remind one of God, but one could not help feeling as if there had been the agency of some – "Mortal Instrument" which Nature had been struggling against without making a perfect conquest.

There was something so wild and new in this feeling, knowing as we did in the inner man that God alone had laid his hand upon it that I could not help regretting the want of it, besides it is a pleasure to a real lover of Nature to give winter all the glory he can, for summer *will* make its own way, and speak its own praises.

Dorothy Wordsworth, *Grasmere Journal*, October 1802

Penhill Beacon and Aysgarth Falls

See beacon'd Penhill, view its stately rise,
Whose scaling altitude invades the skies;
Go, climb its brow, its airy tracks explore,
Where breezes wanton from the western shore;
Freely survey fair Cleveland's distant strand,
And golden Durham's terminating land.
The eye descending now o'er Penhill's base,
We decent Witton's pleasing prospects trace.
Here fleecy troops adorn the sloping green,
There grouping herds diversify the scene;
Now waves voluptuously the pregnant blade
With Bolton's swelling woods of deeper shade;
While the gay buck, as if his hours vain,
Asserts the empire of his active plain;
In rank supreme among the brutal race,
When smoaks his haunch as he inspires the chase
Last in the view, wild surging mountains lie,
That blend their distant summits with the sky.

But now, O Aysgarth, let my rugged verse
The wonders of thy cataracts rehearse.
Long ere the toiling sheets to view appear
They found a prelude to the pausing ear.
Now in rough accents by the pendent wood
Rolls in stern majesty the foaming flood;
Revolving eddies now with raging sway,
To Aysgarth's ample arch incline their way.
Playful and slow the curling circles move
As when soft breezes fan the saving grove;
Till prone again, with tumult's wildest roar,
Recoil the billows, reels the giddy shore;
Dash'd from its rocky bed, the winnow'd spray
Remounts the regions of the cloudy way,
While warring columns fiercer combats join,
And make the rich, rude, thundering scene divine.

Thomas Maude, *Wensleydale – or rural contemplation*, 1780
fourth edition, 1816

A Morning in the Street

Curving and dipping between walled pastures and meadows the moor road sweeps down to the village: a last level stretch, four sentinel larch trees, a precipitous descent, and below, on either hand, houses stand firm against a steep hillside. Here is a moorland approach, a transference of vision from open pasture to clustered habitation, a shock that may be experienced from many other terraces of the Pennines; yet surely few can offer a more sudden change or a more enchanting vista than this at Askrigg Town Head.

At the foot of the hill the high road that for twelve miles has run along the northern slopes of the valley from Leyburn, joins in on the left, and enclosed by buildings takes a sharp bend into the main street. Mounting Elm Hill, a bridge from hillock to hillock between which as we noted the village is squeezed, it curves onwards, hemmed in by stone houses, towards the market-place. A side-turning on the right leads to the West End; a narrow alley, Pudding Lane, slips off to the left, and the road continues steeply downhill, round a corner and up the dale.

The market-place is the hub of our village world. It is not a large area and of no particular shape, yet houses

Askrigg, as seen from the moor road which sweeps down to the village (*Marie Hartley*)

Askrigg in the severe winter of 1947, when the moor road was wall-top high with snow *(watercolour by Marie Hartley)*

surround it pleasantly in the natural way that is the product of gradual growth. Here is the church behind a stout wall, hidden in summer by leafy sycamores; and the cross with a base of five high steps on a wide border of cobble-stones. Here is our shopping centre: two grocers that combine individually green-grocery and cattle food, and jutting out a newspaper and fancy goods shop. Here are the Methodist chapel and the Temperance Hall, the Kings Arms and the Temperance Hotel, but not the Old Hall that for three centuries until 1935 when it was burned down had lent a richness of expression to the scene. Here we hold our celebrations or annual events, pageants and fêtes, band performances and children's sports. Here our few daily buses stop and those for summer outings collect their passengers. None of these is new: there was a church on the same site seven centuries ago, and shops, and an inn known by 'the Signe of the King's Head' before 1700, and as far back as written word records, rejoicings, plays, and sports have been enacted there, and transport of many kinds has halted for a space.

Sheltered from the west wind under the churchyard wall are two summer seats worn smooth by constant use. In the evening they become a meeting-place for the men, the older ones sitting, their pipes alight, the younger ones standing or leaning against the wall, and in the daytime they are occupied by visitors, or a retired mason, a carpenter, or a schoolmaster on holiday at his native village. But in the early hours of a September morning no one is astir; and from them we may watch the first activities of the day.

There is a hushed stillness round about the market-place. On either side of the road that gleams blue-black, damp with few buildings rise abruptly from darkened pavements, and as the light strengthens the stone-work shows up pallid, clear. Their upper windows wide open as if gasping for breath, the houses seem charged with life from their sleeping occupants: gaunt three-storeyed houses, those in the main street lined and creased by age and the stress of living, the sash windows a little askew, the courses not so even as when they were raised stone by stone in the eighteenth century. Their style over-powers that of the dated carved doorways a few of which remain from the previous century, and has so impressed itself on the many buildings of the nineteenth that it is predominant. Burdened with the joys and sorrows of generations of men, they seem temporarily loaned to and not owned by those who will shortly be stirring in them, pursuing their tasks and pleasures, adding their impress by the measure of their sojourn.

The houses are aloof, pride and independence written on their features, and it is they that have moulded the countenance of the village. To some, Askrigg has not altogether a prepossessing face, a shade too stern, lacking the colourful adornment of gardens or that most admired of rural charms a green; yet, more desirable than these, it has character. It bears the imprint of men's skill, of their taste, of constant care, and is the product of environment, and of both farming and industrial growth. The village reflects the rigours of the climate consequent on a situation 700 to 800 feet above sea level, and at the foot of Ellerkin clings to the vast setting with a fitting grace.

Marie Hartley & Joan Ingilby, *Yorkshire Village* (`1953)

A Melancholy Sight

From *Brough*, the road, if I may give it that name, to *Askrigg*, lies over one continuous range of mountains, here called moors. The cultivated vallies are too inconsiderable to deserve a mention. Most of these fifteen miles, however dreadful the road, are tracts of very improveable land; if a good turnpike road was made from *Askrigg* to *Brough*, the first great step to cultivation would be over; for it is almost impossible to improve a country with spirit, the roads of which are impassable. It is extremely melancholy to view such tracts of land that are indisputably capable of yielding many beneficial crops, remaining totally waste, while in many parts of the kingdom farms are so scarce and difficult to procure, that one is no sooner vacant, than twenty applications are immediately made for it.

Arthur Young, *A Six Months Tour Through the North of England*, 1771

Bainbridge and its Horn

From Semerdale, the River Bain enters Bainbridge with a flourish of falling water, a fitting introduction to one of the most spacious and pleasant villages in the dales. The breadth of the green is nicely broken by trees, and the view bounded by the white facade of the Rose and Crown, which pleasingly separates the villages from the more distant fells. By the ancient stocks a small notice-board bears a historical sketch of the village from about A.D. 80, when the Romans built the first of their forts on Brough Hill, a green mound of glacial debris overlooking the village. A road connected with Aldborough (Isurium) near Boroughbridge, and another to the south-west passed over Wether and Cam Fells to link with the Lune valley and with Ribchester, on the Ribble. A southern route flanks Addlebrough and passes by Stalling Busk to Kidstones and Wharfedale. Between Holyrood and Shrovetide, i.e. in autumn and winter, it has long been the custom to sound the Forest Horn each evening, a practice said to date back to Norman times, and intended to guide travellers to the safety of "the towne of Beynbrigge". For many years this has been done by members of the Metcalfe family. Across the way, in The Rose and Crown, a fifteenth century hostelry, one can see the present horn, which hangs in the entrance hall alongside some preserved specimens of trout taken locally ...

It is clear that the good folk of Bainbridge take a pride in their village. Under the trees crocus and snowdrops add a welcome note of colour at the end of winter. Perhaps the finest display is in early May, when masses of jonquils and daffodils bloom on the south side of the green.

Norman Duerden, *Portrait of the Dales*, 1978

Opposite Wensleydale as portrayed by Emma Amsden, a present-day photographer noted for her stunning black-and-white images of the Dales
Top The edge of the storm
Bottom Bolton Castle

The Legend of Semerwater

Where Semerwater now lies, says the legend, there stood some two thousand years ago (some accounts give the actual date as 45 BC) a city of imposing size, with noble buildings and great wealth. To this city there came one day in winter a poor man of venerable appearance who craved an alms at the door of every house in the place, and was driven from each with refusals and reproaches until there was left but one cottage at which he could seek his last chance of succour. Here he met with charity – the cottage folk took him in, fed, warmed and housed him, and made him welcome for the night. Next morning he rose, blessed his entertainers, and set forth on his journey

The still lake of Semerwater under the still skies
Opposite Turner's painting of 1817-18, with the Carling Stone prominent in the foreground *(British Museum)*
Above From virtually the same viewpoint on a cold November day in recent times *(Marie Hartley)*

towards the hills. But when he had arrived on an eminence outside the city he stretched out his arms in malediction crying:

    Semerwater rise
    Semerwater sink
    Swallow all the town
    Save this li'le house
    Where they gave me meat and drink!

Whereupon the earth opened, a great flood of water appeared, and the city of hard hearted folk disappeared, never to be seen again, though it is said that an occasional glimpse of its towers and spires has been seen by curious and fearful watchers who have gazed patiently through its depths.

J. S. Fletcher, *A Picturesque History of Yorkshire*, 1900

The Ballad of Semerwater

Deep asleep, deep asleep,
Deep asleep it lies
The still lake of Semerwater
Under the still skies.

And many a fathom, many a fathom,
Many a fathom below,
In a king's tower and a queen's bower
The fishes come and go.

Once there stood by Semerwater
A mickle town and tall,
King's tower and queen's bower
And the wakeman on the wall.

Came a beggar halt and sore:
" I faint for lack of bread."
King's tower and queen's bower
Cast him forth unfed.

He knocked at the door of eller's cot,
The eller's cot in the dale,
They gave him of their oatcake,
They gave him of their ale.

He has cursed aloud that city proud,
He has cursed it in its pride;
He has cursed it into Semerwater,
Down the brant hillside;
He has cursed it into Semerwater –
There to bide.

King's tower and queen's bower,
And a mickle town and tall;
By glimmer of scale and gleam of fin,
Folk have seen them all.
King's tower and queen's bower
And weed and reed in the gloom;
And a lost city in Semerwater
Deep asleep till doom.

Sir William Watson, *Collected Poems*, 1904

The Wordsworths in Wensleydale - 2

On leaving Askrigg we turned aside to see another waterfall, 'twas a beautiful morning with driving snow-showers that disappeared by fits, and unveiled the east which was all one delicious pale orange colour. After walking through two fields we came to a mill which we pass'd and in a moment a sweet little valley opened before us, with an area of grassy ground, and a stream dashing over various lamina of black rocks close under a bank covered with firs. The bank and stream on our left, another woody bank on our right, and the flat meadow in front from which, as at Buttermere, the stream had retired as it were to hide itself under the shade. As we walked up this delightful valley we were tempted to look back perpetually on the brook which reflected the orange light of the morning among the gloomy rocks with a brightness varying according to the agitation of the current. The steeple of Askrigg was between us and the east, at the bottom of the valley; it was not a quarter of a mile distant, but oh! how far we were from it. The two banks seemed to join before us with a facing of rock common to them both, when we reached this point the valley opened out again, two rocky banks on each side, which, hung with ivy and moss and fringed luxuriantly with brushwood, ran parallel to each other and then approaching with a gentle curve, at their point of union, presented a lofty waterfall, the termination of the valley. Twas a keen frosty morning, showers of snow threatening us but the sun bright and active; we had a task of twenty one miles to perform in a short winter's day, all this put our minds in such a state of excitation that we were no unworthy spectators of this delightful scene. On a nearer approach the water seemed to fall down a tall arch or rather nitch which had shaped itself by insensible moulderings in the wall of an old castle. We left this spot with reluctance but highly exhilarated. When we had walked about a mile and a half we overtook two men with a string of ponies and some empty carts. I recommended to D. to avail herself of this opportunity of husbanding her strength, we rode with them more than two miles, twas bitter cold, the wind driving the snow behind us in the best stile of a mountain storm. We soon reached an Inn at a place called Hardraw, and descending from our vehicles, after warming ourselves by the cottage fire we walked up the brook side to take a view of a *third* waterfall. We had not gone above a few hundred yards between two winding rocky banks before we came full upon it. It appeared to throw itself in a narrow line from a lofty wall of rock; the water which shot manifestly some distance from the rock seeming from the extreme height of the fall to be dispersed before it reached the bason, into a thin shower of snow that was toss'd about like snow blown from the roof of a house. We were disappointed in the cascade though the introductory and accompanying banks were a noble mixture of grandeur and beauty. We walked up to the fall and what would I not give if I could convey to you the images and feelings which were then communicated to me. After cautiously sounding our way over stones of all colours and sizes encased in the clearest ice formed by the spray of the waterfall, we found the rock which before had seemed a perpendicular wall extending itself over us like the ceiling of a huge cave; from the summit of which the water shot directly over our heads into a bason and among fragments of rock wrinkled over with masses of ice, white as snow, or rather as D. says like congealed froth. The water fell at least two yards from us and we stood directly behind it, the excavation not so deep in the rock as to impress any feeling of darkness, but lofty and magnificent, and in connection with the adjoining banks excluding as much of the sky as could well be spared from a scene so exquisitely beautiful. The spot where we stood was as dry as the chamber in which I am now sitting, and the incumbent rock of which the groundwork was limestone veined and dappled with colours which melted into each other in every possible variety. On the summit of the cave were three festoons or rather wrinkles in the rock which ran parallel to each other like the folds of a curtain when it was drawn up; each of them was hung

Chorley, near Askrigg (Marie Hartley)

with icicles of various length, and nearly in the middle of the festoons in the deepest valley made by their waving line the stream shot from between the rows of icicles in irregular fits of strength and with a body of water that momently varied. Sometimes it threw itself into the bason in one continued curve, sometimes it was interrupted almost midway in its fall, and, being blown towards us, part of the water fell at no great distance from our feet like the heavie thunder shower. In such a situation you have at every moment a feeling of the presence of the sky. Above the highest point of the waterfall large fleecy clouds drove over our heads and the sky appeared of a blue more than usually brilliant. The rocks on each side, which, joining with the sides of the cave, formed the vista of the brook were chequered with three diminutive waterfalls or rather, veins of water each of which was a miniature of all that summer and winter can produce of delicate beauty. The rock in the centre of these falls where the water was most abundant, deep black, with, adjoining parts yellow, white, purple, violet and dove colour'd, or covered with water-plants of the most vivid green, and hung with streams and fountains of ice that in some places seemed to conceal the verdure of the plants and the variegated colours of the rocks and in some places to render their hues more splendid. I cannot express to you the enchanted effect produced by this Arabian scene of colour as the wind blew aside the great waterfall behind which we stood and hid and revealed each of these faery cataracts in irregular succession or displayed them with

Wordsworth was entranced when he visited Hardraw Force in 1799, commenting on 'the enchanted effect produced by this Arabian scene of colour'. Turner's watercolour, painted two decades later, captures the grandeur of England's highest unbroken waterfall by stepping back to take a distant view *(Fitzwilliam Museum, University of Cambridge)*

various gradations of distinctness, as the intervening spray was thickened or dispersed. In the luxury of our imaginations we could not help feeding on the pleasure which in the heat of a July noon this cavern would spread through a frame exquisitely sensible. That huge rock of ivy on the right! The bank winding round on the left with all its living foliage, and the breeze stealing up the valley and bedewing the cavern with the faintest imaginable spray. And then the murmur of water, the quiet the seclusions, and a long summer day to dream in! Have I not tired you? With difficulty we tore ourselves away, and on returning to the cottage we found we had been absent an hour. Twas a short one to us, we were in high spirits, and off we drove, and will you believe me when I tell you we walked the next ten miles, by the watch over a high mountain road, thanks to the wind that drove behind us and a good road, in two hours and a quarter, a marvellous feat of which D. will long tell. Well! we rested in a tempting inn, close by Garsdale chapel, a lowly house of prayer in a charming little valley, here we stopp'd a quarter of an hour and then off to Sedbergh 7 miles farther in an hour and thirty five minutes, the wind was still at our backs and the road delightful.

William Wordsworth, *Letter* to Samuel Taylor Coleridge, 24th & 27th December, 1799

Houses Built in Fields

From Hardraw I went westward, and saw a fall of ten feet at a rivlet called Cotter with several small cascades above it. We ascended a hill of the same name, which is very high, our guide guessed from the top down to the Ure 600 yards, but I did not think it so much. We went along the side of this hill, and came to Hellgills, called in the maps Helbeck Lunes; it is a rivlet which rises a little further to the north, and has worn down the rock about twenty feet deep and about four feet in width. It is curious to see the waters run at so great a depth in such a narrow channel, and to step over it. To the east of it is another very small stream, which divides the county of York from the county of Westmoreland, and falls, if I mistake not, into the Hellgills. Hellgill is the rise of the Eden, which falls in at Caerlisle. About half a mile lower there is deep water in it, from which they say the Ure rises, the water going under the ground about a quarter of a mile, and coming out in a field called Lin Park, and they say they have put chaff into the one and it has come out of the other.

About two miles to the north rises the river Swale, a little beyond a natural rock call'd Hugh Seat, and ten or twelve from Apelby. There are no deer in these mountains. The prospect from the height of Cotter is the most awful and grand I ever beheld. The mountains all round, some with their lofty heads at a distance, as Ingleborough and Penigent and the valley beneath, which, tho'it is much narrower to the west of Ascrig, yet it is still a fine vale of good pasturage, and, what is uncommon, there are houses built in most of the fields, which is an unusual prospect, and at a distance make the appearance of scatter'd villages. About Hardrow they find freestone flags, which rise very large, and in them are figures of worms, snakes, and the like, but whether only accidental figures, as such reptiles inclosed, I cannot take upon me to say, but I rather think the former.

On the 24th, leaving this fine dale, we went to the south-west, over the vale in which Widhill Beck runs, having Weather Fell to the right; and ascending up Tenant Hill to the south-east, we had a fine view of the green vale and lofty mountains all round. On this hill we came to some shafts where they had dug for lead. The stones they dug up are of an ash-colour'd marble, and full of trochi and entrochi, and so I observed the rocks were as we went along the mountain. We soon came to Camhill, and near to some cabbins called camhouses, to the north of which are two springs near each other, which soon joyn, and fall into the valley, and then it is called Cam Beck; this they call the rise of the Ribble. In the valley below, a litle to the north of it, is a wet moor, out of which there arises a spring, which is the head of the river Wharfe. A rivlet comes in a short space on each side, and several other afterwards, so that it soon becomes a large river. I observed one of the springs of the Ribble, if I mistake not the southern one, that it incrusts the pebbles with a loose stony matter, which rises up in little columns about half an inch high, and is doubtless caus'd by the stony, coarse particles the water brings along with it, finer particles frequently either petrifying or incrusting with a stone coat.

Richard Pococke, *Journal*, May 31st, 1751

Cotter Force *(Geoff Lund)*

Swaledale

Swaledale is steeper sided and more sinuous than Wensleydale, tinged with the melancholy of vanished industry. Lead-mining flourished in the dale during the eighteenth and nineteenth centuries, and villages were enlarged then. Almost all are on the south facing side of the dale – Healaugh, Low Row, Gunnerside, Muker and Thwaite.

Gunnerside, at the foot of its ravine-like tributary gill, and Muker, at the foot of Kisdon, are memorable in setting and appearance, compact, clustered, clean, always within sound of laughing waters, and sheltered by the friendly hills. Look across to Gunnerside from the Crackpot road south of the river, between a framework of silver birches; admire Muker, or Thwaite, from the Pennine Way track on Kisdon, or less energetically, from the road to Keld, and you'll see the perfect dales landscape of valley, hill, village, stone walls and field barns. Man's contributions are wholly harmonious; even the quarries from which came the splendid sandstone are hidden away in quiet folds of the hills, and most of the lead-mining scars are in remote valleys.

Geoffrey N Wright, *Stone Villages of Britain* 1985

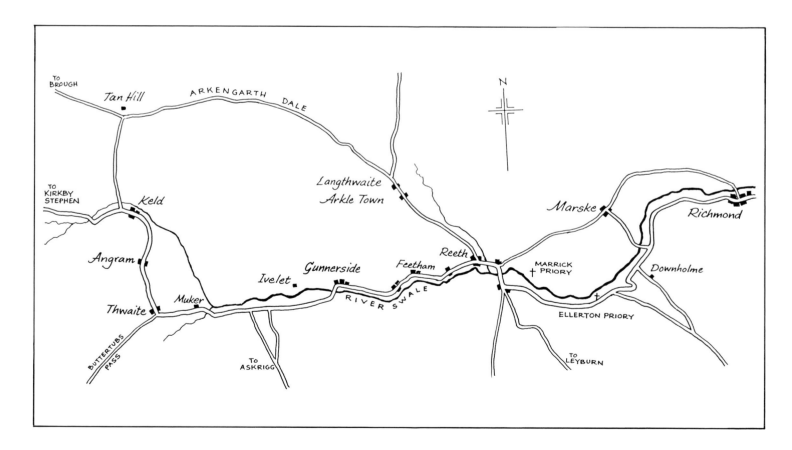

Richmond's spacious Market Place in quieter times. The three storied mid-18th century building, formerly the Blue Bell hotel, became a Woolworths store in 1979

Richmond and the River Swale

This Leades me the ffarthest way to Richmond it being but 8 miles the ready Road from Darlington, but this way is 10 miles and very tedious miles. Three miles off Darlington I passed over Crofton Bridge which crosses ye river Teese which Divides Durham ffrom Yorkshire, and so Entered the North Riding of Yorkshire in which is that they Call Richmondshire a shire of 30 miles. The way was good but Long, I went through Lanes and woods an Enclosed Country; I passed by a house of Sr Mark Melbourn on a hill, a Brick building and severall towers on the top, good gardens and severall rows of trees up to the house, it standing on a hill, ye trees Runns along ye Ridge of ye same - Looks very finely.

Richmondshire has in it 5 waking takes as they Call then, answerable to that they Call hundred in other Countys; Each waking takes has market towns in them and are under a Baliffe Each, which are nominated by the Earle of Holderness who is the Sole Lord of the whole – its 30 miles in Extent. Richmond town one cannot see till just upon it, being Encompass'd w'th great high hills: I descended a very steep hill to it from whence saw the whole town which itself stands on a hill tho' not so high as these by it. Its buildings are all stone, ye streetes are like rocks themselves, there is a very Large space for the Markets w'ch are Divided for the ffish market, the fflesh market, and Corn; there is a Large market Crosse, a square space walled in with severall steps up, and its flatt on the top of a good height. There is by it a Large Church and the ruins of a Castle, the pieces of the walls on a hill. I walked round by the walls, the River running beneath a great descent to it, its full of stones and Rocks and soe very Easye to Make or keep up their wires or falls of water, which in some places is naturall ye water falls over Rocks with great force which is Convenient for Catching Salmon by spere when they Leap over those Bayes. All rivers are Low and Dryer in summer, soe I saw them at the greatest disadvantage being in some places almost drye and the Rockes and stones appear bare, but by those high and large stone bridges I pass'd which lay across the Rivers showed the Great Depth and breadth they used to be in ye Winter tymes. There was two good houses in ye town, one was Mr Dareys the Earl of Holderness' brother, the other was Mr Yorkes, both stood then were chosen Parliament men. They had good gardens walled in, all stone, as in the whole town, though I must say it Looks Like a sad shatter'd town and fallen much to Decay and Like a Disregarded place.

Celia Fiennes, *Through England on a Side Saddle*, 1690s

Sir Solomon Swale

The town of Richmond (Cambden calls it a city) is wall'd, and had a strong castle; but as those things are now slighted, so really the account of them is of small consequence, and needless; old fortifications being, if fortification was wanted, of very little significance; the river Swale runs under the wall of this castle, and has some unevenness at its bottom, by reason of rocks which intercept it passage, so that it falls like a cataract, but not with so great a noise.

The Swale is a noted river, though not extraordinary large, for giving name to the lands which it runs through for some length, which are called Swale Dale, and to an antient family of that name, one of whom has the vanity, as I have heard, to boast, that his family was so antient as not to receive that name from, but to give name to the river it self. One of the worthless successors of this line, who had brought himself to the dignity of what they call in London a Fleeter, used to write himself, in his abundant vanity, Sir Solomon Swale, of Swale Hall, in Swale Dale, in the county of Swale, in the North Riding of York.

The addition of *dale*, first given here to the low lands about the head of the Swale, is grown up into a custom or usage from all the rivers which rise in those western hills north of this, quite to and into Scotland; for example,

Teesdale for the River Tees.
Wierdale for the Wier which runs through Durham.
Tine Dale for the Tine, which runs to Newcastle.
Tweedale for the Tweed, which passeth by Berwick.
Clydsdale, Nydsdale, and many others.

Daniel Defoe, *Tour through the Whole Island of Great Britain*
(Letter VIII), 1724

Richmond castle and bridge from across the Swale, as painted by Edmund John Niemann in 1867
(Tennants Auctioneers)

Swaledale at its most dramatic, viewed from Moor Close above Thwaite as storm clouds gather down the valley *(Marie Hartley)*

Undiscovered Swaledale

The valley above Richmond presents at the present day an aspect not wholly unlike what it wore when the Norman earl first explored its rocks and woods. Till within a few years ago, there was no proper road up the valley, the usual way to Reeth being over the bare hill by the racecourse. The road opened eleven years since is more fortunately directed, generally along the sides of the valley, which it crosses twice before arrival at Reeth. At the moment we write there is no public conveyance on this route. Perhaps the Railway Company might advantageously supply for the summer months this deficit, which is much to be lamented as shutting out one of the most beautiful tracts in the country from all but individuals with strong limbs or long purses.

Wishing our readers may have one or other of these qualifications, or that he may find this petition of mine to the able managers of the railway answered by a smart "Reeth and Swaledale Bus" at the Richmond Station, we will turn our face westward, and descend from the rock on which the town is built, only looking back now and then to notice the good effect, in a pictorial sense, of the old-looking but really modern tower, called the Temple, which stands on a pleasant hill, a little to the west of the great tower of the castle. Forward the dale begins to show its many sinuosities, promontories, and hollows most enriched by ancient wood, alternatively adhering to and returning from the stream. Beyond the mill we remark a singular round hill, crowned with trees, which stands on the centre of a semicircular sweep of the high, woody cliff.

The artist may observe in these woody escarpments two distinct beds of limestone rock, which for twenty miles up the dale appear again and again, always rising higher and higher, and always important to the geologist, as a constant mark in his sections, and to the miner as the most productive repositories of lead ore.

Arrived at the bridge, by which the road is carried to the south side of the river, we look forward on the right to a lofty hill, above which the old road runs, and on the left to a bold promontory, beneath the unseen village of Hudswell. Winding round this rugged promontory, below woods and rocks, the road opens continually new and pleasing views, in which no trace of man is visible, except where, below us, the philosophic bearer of the rod is trying to deceive the trout. These woods, in spring, are full of shrill music, softened by the cooing of doves, and occasionally startled by the scream of some jealous or clamorous vocalist. Nor is the pleasure at all lessened from a point somewhere further in the road; we look back on the oak, ash, elm and sycamore, the dark holly, the darker yew, and white-blossomed bird cherry, which diversify the broad surface of this rocky hill. Now few of my northern friends know, and how few of my southern friends have ever heard, that so fair a scene of natural beauty lies so near the proud Earl Conan's Tower. And yet we feel not half its beauty, unless, like the angler or the artist, we thread the margin of the sinuous stream, listen to its everlasting murmur, and catch the innumerable happy accidents of light and shade which escape from its rugged and shaded bank.

John Phillips, *Excursions in Yorkshire by the North Eastern Railway*, 1853

Keld and its Chapel

Keld was the site of a Norse settlement and the name can be related to the word 'Appeltekelda' meaning the spring near the apple tree. If we go back to 12,000BC we learn that a glacier moving down Swaledale left a moraine above what is now Keld and this changed the course of the River. The site of the village may originally have been an island and there is evidence that the River then flowed down to the west of Kisdon Hill, passed the present village of Thwaite and then on to Muker. However as a result of the moraine, the Swale forced a channel through the limestone strata making the new course between Kisdon and Beldi Hill on the way to Muker. This change of course is thought to have created the Catrake and the impressive Kisdon Falls. At one time Keld was a busy village standing at the head of Swaledale. It has a school, public house, a village hall, and shops. According to Leland there was a chapel at Keld in 1530 but history related that, following a riot, it had to be closed. There was probably disputes among the local inhabitants about the Dissolution of the monasteries.

Certainly, by 1789, it was in a ruinous state and was rebuilt only because of the efforts of a preacher named Edward Stillman. He walked all the way to London to raise £700 for the rebuilding, spending only sixpence during his travels and returning to Keld with the money he had collected. He remained as minister in Keld for forty-eight years. The chapel however had no burial ground. Today the population of Keld has dwindled, there is still a chapel, but no school or public house, and the quiet of the village is broken only by the walkers who pass through and stay at the local Youth Hostel.

David Morris, *The Swale – A History of the Holy River of St Paulinus* 1994

Swaledale's Tide of Colour

When the sun shines no spot is more welcoming, no paths more inviting than those by the river banks across flower-filled meadows, through green and shadowy woods in deep gorges, rounding the slopes of lovely hills like Kisdon. Even the confirmed motorist who stays in Muker becomes enthralled and discovers there is more in this 'countrygoing lark' than just passing up and down dales in cars.

A spring morning, sun chasing across fell and dale, breezes tossing green boughs and scattering blossom in showers white and pink: this is a day for Kisdon, for mounting its rounded shoulders, birds blown screaming across our path, mountain pansies and purple orchises in our way, and as we stop to look around every upward yard raises up more heavenly ridges and ranges, each changing from blue to gold as sungleams and cloud shadows race over them. Or when the dale floor paths please me best, across the flower-filled June or early July meadows before the hay cutter mows down swathes of dark-headed burnet, creamy pignut, meadowsweet and campions, pale pink bistort and dark crimson clover heads, and drifts of blue and purple, deep cerise and red cranesbill. Only Tyrolean slopes are more thickly set with flowers then those above Swale in midsummer, or in late spring when the low pastures are awash with bluebells, the tide of colour flowing into the hazel copses and invading the very sides of Kisdon and Swinnergill.

Jessica Lofthouse, *A Countrygoer in the Dales*, 1964

Above Upper Swaledale near Keld, with the rounded shoulders of Kisdon on the left of the picture *(Simon Warner)*

Left Shaw Farm, Arkengarthdale *(Marie Hartley)*

Nidderdale

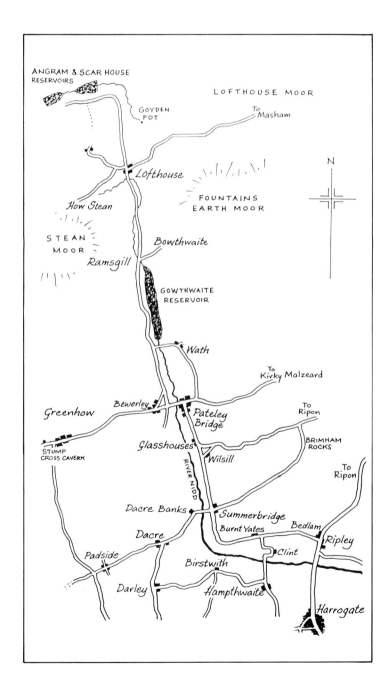

Pateley Bridge lies deep in Nidderdale at a bridging place where the old monastic route from Fountains Abbey to Grassington and Kilnsey crosses the old valley route proceeding up the dales and thence to Masham and Wensleydale via Lofthouse. It also formed a link between the former industrial villages and hamlets and the seemingly remote countrysides of the upper dale. The place-name refers to 'pate' or badger and just across the river is Bewerley, a name associated with the beaver, showing how wild this area may have been in Saxon times. Pateley gained a market in the fourteenth century and since then it has had a varied history. It probably did not amount to very much in medieval times, for early in the sixteenth century it was a focus for the local flax and linen industry, whilst the association with lead-mining goes back at least to Roman times. At the end of the eighteenth century the market was still flourishing and in 1794 the Board of Agriculture surveyors reported that Pateley was 'a fine thriving place.' In addition to the town's butchering and linen industries they mention the export of salted butter and hams to London (the meat being too lean for the Lancashire trade) and the sale of hogs fattened on oatmeal to the Lancashire mill towns. Within a few decades, however, the market was in decline and Pateley was finding salvation in lead-mining and quarrying. Had a scheme in 1820 come to fruition Pateley and Knaresborough would have shared the first public railway in England, which was planned to handle quarrying and flax/linen products. It was not until 1849 that parliamentary approval was granted for a Nidderdale line to Pateley Bridge and not until 1860 that work began. It was completed in 1862 at a cost of £8000 per mile. Then, between 1904 and 1908, a light railway was built from

Pateley Bridge - 'a shopping and recreational centre which still just manages to avoid being twee'. Tarmac has now replaced cobbles in the main street and, sadly, the Bay Horse Inn on the left was demolished in 1957 to make way for a car park

Pateley to the head of the dale at Angram, where two reservoirs were being built. With the completion of Scar House in 1936 the light railway was demolished, whilst the Nidd Valley line closed to passengers in 1951 and to goods in 1964. These railways opened up Nidderdale to the first trickle of tourism, but there can be no doubt that were they to exist today then Pateley would be a major centre of tourism in the Dales. As it is, the town is a local shopping and recreational centre which still just manages to avoid being twee. The core of the town consist of a straight and narrow sloping High Street lined by shops, some of which are now of much more interest to visitors than to locals. But nobody could deny the picturesque quality of the scene. The townlet is noted for its remarkable summer displays of hanging baskets. and after the threat

of frost recedes at the start of June the proprietors vie to produce the finest floral displays. The most evocative feature of Pateley is, however, missed by most visitors and consist of the ruins of the Church of St Mary sited high above the townlet. A chapel was established here before 1321 and from the ruins of the medieval church one has a fine view of the valley, Pateley and the replacement of St Mary's. Pateley folk were far too canny not to take advantage of a grant made available in 1818 for the building of new churches in parishes with more than 4000 inhabitants but church space for less than 1000.

All who have made the steep uphill slog to St Mary's will understand why the decision was taken to build anew rather than to repair and enlarge the old church.
Richard Muir, *The Dales of Yorkshire* 1991

Brimham Rocks

Brimham Rocks are scattered over some fifty acres on Brimham Moor, and present a great variety of weird and fantastic shapes, amid which the guide will point out gigantic mimic heads of elephant, hippopotamus and porpoise, as well as dancing bears, mushrooms, "Druids' sacrificial basins", "Druids' reading desks", "oyster shells", and as the visitors become more intimate they are introduced to "kissing chairs" and "lovers' leaps". Like the stacks at Plumpton these are due to some original difference of resistance to weathering, though the geologist may confess a suspicion that Art has occasionally aided Nature where her hand has faltered in an evident purpose. It was in the Eighteenth Century that these monster curiosities first sprang to fame, and that was an epoch when any little defect or inelegance in Nature was readily remedied by the landscape-gardener. The natural isolation of the stacks is much more complete than at Plumpton, and the undercutting, which

Above Brimham Rocks, where fantastic shapes have been created by the power of wind erosion *(Geoff Lund)*

Left Hawthorn berries bring a touch of autumn to the view of Gouthwaite Reservoir from above Wath *(Simon Warner)*

is so marked a feature, seems to be largely due to wind-erosion. On a very small scale wind-erosion may still be seen in process here, but in the declining stage of the Glacial Period, when the exposed land-surfaces would have but a very scanty cover of vegetation, wind-erosion must have been much more effective. Every gale of wind would drive the detached particles of the Millstone Grit before it; they would not rise high, but they would affect deeply every exposed rock-face within a foot or two of the general level of the country. The same effect exactly is observed in the Libyan Desert and about the Pyramids, but the exceedingly sharp grains of the Millstone Grit have vastly more cutting power than the rounded grains of the Desert sands. Hence has arisen much of the undercutting of the stones at Brimham, and the particularly characteristic horizontal fluting at and a little above the ground level.

Percy Fry Kendall and Herbert E. Wroot, *Geology of Yorkshire* 1924.

How Stean Gorge

The How Stean Beck, which runs through a little valley of its own, has its source in many rills, cutting the slopes of Whernside successively through the measures of Millstone Grit, the Yoredale shales, plates, sandstones, &c. down to the Lower Scar limestone. It has often been compared with the deep and gloomy canyons of the North America Continent, but although the peculiar and of course much smaller channel of How Stean has been produced in a similar manner to the mighty, arid ravines of Colorado, the resulting scenery of the Nidderdale canyon is infinitely more pleasing and picturesque. Owing to the excessive summer heat and the almost entire absence of rain, there is an utter dearth of animal and vegetable life; not a tree, bird or creature of any kind being visible. On the other hand the gorge of How Stean lies amid a wealth of foliage, presenting a great variety of beautiful and luxuriant scenes. In some places the ravine is nearly 80 feet deep, richly draped with mosses, ivy, wild flowers, and spreading trees. Many choice ferns likewise grow in the crevices of the steep faces of the rock, happily out of reach of the ruthless collector. Rustic bridges span the chasm high above the sounding stream, and at one part of it a narrow path, protected by a hand-rail, has been formed along its bank, by which the visitor is enabled to penetrate the whole extent of the gorge, and leisurely view the magnificent scenery which displays fresh beauties at every turn.

Harry Speight, *Upper Nidderdale* 1906

Part 2

People
and the
Landscape

Sheep above Reeth in Swaledale *(painting by Robert Nicholls)*

Farming and the Farming Community

The Great Fair on Malham Moor

... a prodigious large field of enclosed land, being upwards of 732 acres in one pasture, a great part of which is a fine, rich soil and remarkable for making cattle both expeditiously and uncommonly fat. This GREAT CLOSE properly so called was for many years rented by Mr Birtwhistle of Skipton, the celebrated Craven Grazier, and on which you might frequently see 5,000 head of Scotch Cattle at one time. As soon as these were a little freshened, notice was dispersed among the neighbouring markets and villages, that a great FAIR would be held in this Field on a particular day, and lots being separated by guess as nearly as could such manner be done to the wants and wishes of any Purchaser, so much was fixed immediately by the eye upon that lot, of so much per head, taking them as they were accidentally intermixed upon an average. To a stranger this mode of bargaining will appear exceedingly difficult and precarious; but it is amazing with what readiness and exactitude persons accustomed to the business will ascertain the value of a very large lot, frequently of several hundreds together.

As soon as these were disposed of, a fresh Drove succeeded; and beside Sheep and Horses frequently great in numbers, Mr Birtwhistle has had Twenty Thousand head of Cattle on the field in one summer; every Herd enticed from their native soil and ushered into this fragrant Pasture, by the Pipe of an Highland Orpheus.

If the Craven Graziers will yet esteem it a benefit to the Country, Mr Birtwhistle has the merit of being the first who traversed the Hebrides and the Isles and Counties in the North of Scotland, and that at hazardous period, in 1745, beginning a Commerce, which by gradual increase ever since seems to have checked the ancient breeding the LONG HORNED Craven Cattle, which were formerly held in highest estimation. And even yet, although the price of the Scots are becoming extravagantly high, the Trade continues to wait on its highest vigour.

... Mr B. has had 10,000 head in cattle on the road from Scotland at one time. Vast quantities are fed in every part of Craven for the markets in the populous towns both in Yorkshire and Lancashire.

Thomas Hurtley, *A Concise Account of Some Curiosities in the environs of Malham*, 1786

Longhorn cattle at the head of Bishopdale. This ancient breed would be familiar to 18th century drovers converging on Malham Moor for their 'Great Fair' (*Geoff Lund*)

Building the Drystone Walls
and Burning the Lime

The ride (to Malham) is truly wild and romantic; nature here sits in solitary grandeur on the hills, which are lofty, green to the top, and rise in irregular heaps on all hands, in their primeval state of pasture, without the least appearance of a plough, or habitation, for many miles. In the summer they afford good keep for cattle, great numbers of which are taken in to feed from April or May to Michaelmas, when the owners generally choose to take them away. The pasturage if a horse for that time is 14s; a cow 7s; a sheep 1s 6d. Many of these pastures, which are of great extent, have been lately divided by stone walls, of about two yards high, one yard wide at the bottom, lessening to a foot at the top. A man can make about seven yards, in length, of this in one day, and is paid from 20d to 2s. The stone brought and laid down from him, cost about 7s more.

. . . The stone of the hills around Maum, is burnt into lime, of which five pecks, each containing 16 quarts, are delivered at the kiln mouth for 7d. It takes a week in burning and when it begins to be calcined, the lowest stratum is drawn out of the mouth, and more stone and coal put in at the top.

William Bray, *Sketch of a Tour into Derbyshire and Yorkshire*, 1777
second edition 1783

Wharfedale waller Geoff Lund, who took many of the photographs in this book, building a new stretch of wall above Conistone. This view shows well the arrangement of throughs, fillings and topstones *(David Morgan Rees)*

Sheep Washing

I was once at a sheep-washing where the old farmers grew so hilarious and boisterous that they threw a meddlesome village cobbler into the muddy pool, when the man standing there, almost armpit deep, solemnly washed him and then thrust him under, just as a moment before he had treated a grizzled old ram. It was a sort of tradition amongst sheep washers that nothing alcoholic should be consumed whilst a man stood armpit deep in the pool, because the spirit was supposed to go no farther down inside the body than the water mounted outside, and thus easily affected one's head. I cannot say whether there is any truth in the assertion or not, because in my farming days I was a total abstainer. Anyhow, standing for over an hour on end in cold spring water was a trying business. I remember, when I was a lad of nineteen, washing sheep so long in a pool formed by damning a mountain beck that, upon emerging, I was too benumbed to undress myself, and this had to be done for me by friends. The weather was particularly cold for the season and showers of hail were from time to time striking like bird-shot the surface of the pool wherein I stood.

Richard Kearton, *A Naturalist's Pilgrimages*   1926

Sheep washing at Sigsworth, Upper Nidderdale, in 1914
(Ben McKenzie collection)

Sheep at Keld, rounded up for washing their white faces *(**Marie Hartley**)*

Ennis Bentham of Docklesyke Farm, Deepdale, out on the tops in the depths of winter looking for buried sheep (*John & Eliza Forder*)

Shepherds and their Dogs

The eyes of a sheepdog are his greatest asset. He must be able to see quickly and to be able to eye (control) the sheep. It is possible to have too much "eye", known as hard eye, which means that the dog may be excellent when concentrating on a few sheep but cannot control a large flock. Dogs that eye early are not always the best in the end. Those that start at a year are often better. Unfortunately, sometimes a dog may work splendidly for a few years and then suddenly go right off.

Yet Maddie, Mr Lancaster's ten-year-old bitch, "a great dog", had won seven trials before she was eighteen months old. "She has it in her. Put her on the fell and away she goes, she's in her element." Full of sheepdog lore, he told us the most difficult manoeuvre to teach is to "learn 'em to flank, to keep their distance from sheep and to go quietly. The quieter you and dog are the better.

Don't issue too many commands, and you yourself must have sheep sense." Both Tom Lancaster and Laurie Peacock always found bitches more sensitive to commands than dogs, but on the whole dogs are more popular and many people consider them to be more even in their work than bitches.

Three gifts which are born in a dog cannot be taught. The first is to be able to recognise a wanted sheep and to single it out from a flock; the second is to be able to single out his owners' sheep from those of neighbours', which is useful, but can be awkward if you want to bring in strays; the third is to be able to set sheep burying in snow drifts, although an old dog, who could set, has been known to reach young ones. To do this the dog stands rigid on scenting the sheep.

Mr Lancaster had a wonderful dog called Fan who

could set sheep. In one very bad storm he lost 203 sheep, but would have lost three or four hundred but for her. "She set 'em," he said, "thirty feet down; she was as true as steel. She would walk on top of the drifts, all at once stop and *whinge* a little, and we would dig and find em." Dogs cannot set dead sheep, which sometimes lie on top of live ones so that some may be missed.

For two periods of seven and eleven years Mr Thomas Joy was the shepherd in charge of 1,000 sheep on Grassington Moor. "I had three good dogs – Lass, Lady and Scot. Lass was three years old before she was trained, and I never let her near the sheep for a month at first. She was always on the go *tittering* about, covering the moor twice over."

In one of the storms of the winter of 1947 George Capstick, then managing his mother's farm in Howgill, started out with the farm servant at 9 a.m. on to the hill to gather. "It takes a good man an hour to walk to the top of the fell". They were returning with the flock in mist and snow, when suddenly the mist cleared and they saw four wethers. He loosed his dog, Ken, who set off to fetch them. Then the mist closed down again. They knew if they made enough noise that Ken would know where they were. But at the Fell Gate there was no Ken, and about 5.45 p. m. they returned to the farm to milk. At night he and his mother, who sat knitting "with her knitting sheath and old bent needles", listened to the nine o'clock news. "What do you say if we go up to the Fell Gate?" he asked. Looking over her spectacles his mother replied: "Yes, it's a good idea." He and the man, taking a torch and lantern, set out. As they approached the Fell Gate they saw a sparkle. "Them's sheep's eyes," he cried, and there were the four wethers. Beside them deep in the snow, with a drift a foot high on his back, lay Ken. He could have left them and come home but he hadn't. "There's loyalty for you. I'm always thankful I went up to the Fell Gate."

If there is real understanding between you and your dog, it will pull that last bit out to help you, but in the end of course it depends on the individual dog and on its pluck. So there they are: Ben, Bob, Laddie, Lassie, Fly, Hemp, Moss, Nell, Tiger, Toss, Wiley and all the rest of them, quietly going about their masters' business on moor and fell, day after day, year in, year out.

Marie Hartley and Joan Ingilby, *Life and Tradition in the Yorkshire Dales*, 1968

Dale Farm in Spring

(for Ella Pontefract and Marie Hartley)

T'GROUND rises brantly to nor'east,
Wi' t'walls zigzagging ower t'intake –
T'walls 'at wur builded first by t'Danes,
Girt dry-steean walls. Noo lambkins laik
In t'greenin' pastures. Ragged ewes
Crop steadily an' niver heed
T'lambs carryin'-ons. A galloway
Whinnies whenever folk leave t'stead.

Thro t'peartree-flowers, t'hills are deep-blue
An' violet; thoo coudn't match
Ther colour wi' nowt save a plum.
Below t'front door ther is a patch
of taties, an' half hid by birks
A river runs wi' mony a twist
To peaty pools; when t'wind is low,
When t'rooks in yonder crow-prate whist

An' motor-buses stop ther din,
thro' t'windows thoo can hear its sang.
Lile birds cheep oot of brokken shells
An' curlew whistle t'whole day long.

A white hen wi' her primrose chicks
Chuffs proudly ower t'daisied grass,
Cluckin' to folk abooot her brood:
T'cock watches 'em, as bold as brass.
Black Border Nell has four more pups
Sich bonnie handfuls wi' blue eyes.
A new-born calf bleats in a byre:
A cuckoo calls ayont a rise
Of larches. 'Luve ! coom thi ways in,'
T'winter wur lang an' lingering,
'We'd never thol it,' farmwife says,
'Save for our hopes o' t'commin' spring.'

Dorothy Una Ratcliffe

A matchless study of a shepherd and his dog by Bertram Unne. Raymond Peel was photographed at Redshaw Hall Farm, West End, complete with the customary crook made from hazel

Haytime

... The grass being strewed equally, and laid as light on the ground as possible, is suffered to remain in that condition until next day, about eleven o'clock, when the upper surface of the grass will be found dried and withered; the hay-makers then begin at the side of the field furthest from the wind, and make the grass into small rows, which, if artfully performed, will expose an entirely new surface of the grass to the influence of the sun and air: this operates with great facility. In the evening of the same day, the rows are made into small cocks ("foot cocks"); the next morning, as soon as the dew is well evaporated, the cocks are spread abroad carefully by the hand; about noon, when thought necessary, it is again made into small rows, called turnings, which, by varying the surface, expedite its complete drying; and if the weather has been perfectly fine from the cutting of the grass it is found sufficiently dry to carry it to the barn, or rick, if the quantity to be put together is not very great; but if that is the case, it is sometimes made into large cocks, but it is never allowed to remain long before it is carried, as the base of the cock would be injured by the moisture of the ground, as well as the outside influence of the weather.

In the dales, when the above method of hay-making is practised, there is scarcely an acre in tillage. Hay is the grand object of the farmer, and he bestows upon it the most sedulous attention, and has many difficulties to combat: the season commences late, the surrounding hills occasion frequent and sudden showers, and the meadows, which are all natural, abound with the *trifolium repens* . . . etc; which being more succulent than the grasses properly so called, are more difficult to harvest than the produce of meadows where the grasses greatly predominate; yet with all the difficulties, more hay is reaped in these dales with the same number of hands, than any other place I have seen.

William Fothergill of Carr End

Tukes's *General View of the Agriculture of the North Riding of Yorkshire* 1800

Haymaking

Now it was tea-time, and we had tea served after the Wensleydale manner – plain cakes and currant cakes, cakes hot and cold, and butter and cheese at discretion, with liberty to call for 'anything else that you like' and the more you eat and drink, the more you will rise in the esteem of your hospitable entertainers. And after that I went down to the hayfield, for it was a large field, and the farmer longed to get the hay all housed before sunset.

They don't carry hay in the dales, they "lead" it and the two boys from Oxfordshire were not a little proud in having the "leading" assigned to them, seeing that they had nothing to do but ride the horse that drew the hay-sledge to and fro between the barn and the "wind-rows".

Another difference is that forks are not used except to pitch the hay from the sledge to the barn, all the rest – turning the swath, making it into cocks – is done with the rake and by hand. So I took a rake, and beginning at one side of the field at the same time with an old hand, worked away so stoutly, that he had much ado to keep ahead of me. And so it went on, all hands working as if there were no such thing as weariness, load after load slipping away to the barn; and I unconsciously growing meritorious.

"You're the first cockney I ever saw," said the stalwart farmer, "that knew how to handle a rake." Had I stayed with him a week, he would have discovered other of my capabilities equally praiseworthy. We should have

Haymaking at Nessfield, near Bolton Abbey, painted by noted local artist Herbert Royle *(Tennants Auctioneers)*

accomplished the task and cleared the field; but a black cloud rose in the west, and soon sent down a heavy shower, and compelled us to huddle up the remaining rows into cocks, and leave them till morning.....The hay harvest is an exciting time in the dales, for grass is the only crop, and the cattle had to be fed all through the long months of winter and sometimes far into a backward spring. Hence everything depends on the hay being carried and housed in good condition; and many an anxious look is cast at passing clouds and distant hill-tops to learn the signs of the weather. The dalesmen are expert in the use of the scythe; and a number of them, after their own haymaking is over, migrate into Holderness and other grain-growing districts, and mow down the crops, even the wheat-fields, with remarkable celerity.

Walter White, *A Month in Yorkshire*, 1858

Above The Fothergill family of Riddings, Howgill, turning hay in rows, about 1940 *(Kenneth Shepherd)*
Opposite Memories! There can be few more evocative Dales photographs than these two views of hayfield 'drinkings' - the Middleton family of Deepdale *(top: Geoffrey N. Wright);* and the Harkers of Crackpot Hall, Swaledale *(bottom: Marie Hartley)*

Haytime

I would show you them -
The hills - through my eyes today
With the folk in the meadows strewing,
Strewing the hay,
Rhythmically moving up and down.
I would send the sheer breath of the country
To you in the town.
White gulls are dipping,
Soaring out there on the breeze
Over crested grass like waves rippling
In warm summer seas.
O! I would send you these today -
The peace of the hills, and sweet on the wind
The scent of the hay.

Joan Ingilby, *Poems*, 1984

(wood engraving by Marie Hartley)

The Condition of the Poor

There was an old custom in bygone days of dividing the common lands of every village into patches of various sizes, called in this part of Yorkshire "reins" or "reeans". It is thought that these terraces, which are seen in the vicinity of our villages, must have been levelled for this purpose, and used for the cultivation of their crops, such as flax, and lint, potatoes or oats. Each member of the community held one or more of these strips of land for three years, and it then changed hands. But it was not helpful to the improvement of the land, for naturally every holder was anxious to get as much good out of the land as he possibly could during his short tenure of it, and the Acts of Enclosure, passed in 1836 and subsequently, and the laying down of much of the arable land into pasture, all helped to diminish the work for the population, and so reduce their numbers, and send them off to help crowd the cities ...

In the old days, intercourse even with their nearest neighbour was very exceptional; no one except the farmer moved about, and he chiefly to Skipton or Long Preston fairs on horseback. Indeed sixty years ago there was only a single "gig" in the parish – belonging to Mr Knowles of Halton Gill. They were very self-contained, they had not even an occasional visit from a butcher, a privilege much esteemed these days – and the price of mutton in 1836 was only 4d a pound! The farmers killed and salted a pig or two, and usually a large piece of "a slaughtered ox" was dried and salted, and hung up in the chimney-nook of the house. Close by were cakes and riddlebread hanging. But the oatcake making is dying out even in the farmhouses. As for the labourer and the farm-servant (though he usually lived in the farmhouse, and fared well) they seldom had any fresh butcher's meat; and one year, when the vicar gave a piece of mutton to a labourer at Christmas, he said "Thank you, sir: I have had none since that bit you gave me last Christmas." Porridge, tea and oatcake was their usual fare.

Ven. Archdeacon Boyd, "Fifty years in Arncliffe" from *Littondale Past and Present*, 1893

Baking Oatcake

These cakes are made of oatmeal and water or buttermilk or, what is termed blue milk – that is, milk after the cream has been skimmed off it, but very unlike the blue milk of London, to which the Water Companies' cows, the *pumps*, so mainly contribute. A regular baker of these cakes can "turn-off" thirty in an hour – a peck of oatmeal, containing twenty eight pounds, will make sixty five cakes, for the baking of which eight pence is charged, and the price of the cake is wholly dependent upon the market price of meal.

The meal is generally mixed the night before baking in the *kneading-tub*, one hand continually stirring the mixture to prevent any lumps whilst the other is employed putting in the meal. This tub, which is kept expressly for the purpose, is rarely ever cleansed with water, but merely partially scraped out with a knife. – The particles adhering to the sides ferment, and cause the next quantity of meal put into the tub to rise more speedily....

On the morning of baking, the *backstone* (formerly a slate but now invariably a plate of iron let into a framework of bricks over a stove) is thoroughly cleansed – a fire is lighted at a mean temperature – near to it a table is placed and the meal ready for use. The baker, with a snow-white apron and unimpeachable hands, having ascertained the

Making oatcake - an illustration from *The Costume of Yorkshire* by George Walker (1814)

heat of the backstone, commences operations, and you cannot well conceive what a field there is for exercise of grace.

A flat piece of wood, about seventeen inches square with lines scored upon it crossways, called a *backboard*, is sprinkled with some dry meal – the hand is then moved over the surface of the board in a circular direction, leaving an area of meal in the centre, upon which a ladle-full from the kneading tub is poured. The board being lifted off the table, is shaken with both hands, and the meal obeying the rotary motion, spreads in circular form-this is transferred to a piece of thin linen, or at times cartridge paper, called the "*turning-off*" resting on a smooth board

called a *spittle*, very similar to the backboard in shape. having the addition of a handle and an edge of iron; the cake is then with a strong jerk thrown laterally upon the backstone and the linen is taken up: this movement requires great dexterity, and the length of the cake proves the efficiency of the baker. After baking for a minute, the spittle is put in request in turning it – another minute completes the baking, and the cake is placed on one of the backs of the "fleeok" its shape being oval in form and half to three quarters of a yard long; it is much eaten, and considered very wholesome.

Frederic Montagu, *Gleanings in Craven*, 1838

117

Gayle Bannock

Some spots er nooated fer watter en sand.
Some spots er nooated fer scenery ets grand,
Some spots er nooated fer makken ya fit,
There's a spot cawd Gayle whar bannocks tha'it.

Bannocks er meead i ' Scotland, the' say,
Wi' ooatmeal er barley meal, either way,
But there meead wi' fluer like pasties et Gayle,
Ther meead bi' wimmin ets t'best cooks int' dale.

There's bannocks en bannocks ez ivveryyan knaas,
Some's meed i' Dent en some meead at Haas,
Ther aw different, it' s watter the' say,
T'best's meead at Gayle, its true awaywa.

Some's meead wi' currens en some just plain,
Some's thick, some's thin, ther aw reet ez rain,
Some's square, some's roond, there aw makks en shapps,
Some's lile, but some er ez big ez coo claps.

When men wrought et t' quarry, the 'wer up wi't' lark,
The' aw tuke some bannock in ther tins te wark,
"It fills yer belly, it's grand," says Rannock,
"There's nowt y 'it ets better ner bannock."

Bannock sud bend afoor the brek, the'say,
Tha's better bi tufe than crummle away.
"A want neea fancy stuff," said Mike,
"Just gi me a bannock ah knaa what a like."

Some like poddish, en some like breead,
Some like trotters, er hauf a sheeps heead,
My favrite's a bannock ets mead at Gayle,
For fillen a hooal it nivver does fail.

Some's fond a bacon, some's fond a meeat,
Some's fond of eggs, ther gay bad ta beeat,
Some's fond of a sausage, some's fond of a chop,
But I'se fond of a bannock wi treacle ont' top.

Some's fond o cabbage, some's fond o' peeas,
Some's fond o pasty, some's fond o' cheese,
Some's fond o ceeaks, some's fond of spice,
But Gaylites like bannock, they knaa what's nice.

A bannock gat foisty in a dairy int' Becksteeans,
A woman threw it oot along wi' some beeans,
It landed int' beck, a guse et it aw,
T'guse sank int't dub doon bit't 'waterfaw.

A Gayle chap tuke a bannock te France in the war,
He ran oot o amminition, it had happened before.
He tuke out his bannock, he threw it insteead,
Ther wez twenty Germans liggen like deead.

When I gat hitched tev a lass frae a toon,
Wa walked ya neet i' the light o' the moon,
I ast her a question, twas neea time te jest,
"Can ye beeak a Gayle bannock ?" This was the test.

There was yance a chap et wez gaen te dee,
"A pirned to deeath, az famished," said he.
"Gi me a bannock, if its last thing a see,
Al bi satisfied than, al bi reddy te dee."

Gayle Bannock: 2lb of flour, 1lb of lard, current or raisins,
water (no milk)

James Alderson

Mrs J Alderson of Keld using a spittle and bakstone to make havercake - a North Riding variant of oatcake (*Marie Hartley*)

Horses played a dominant role in farm life in the Dales until as late as the 1950s. A scene such as this at Grassington smithy, with the farrier shoeing a horse as the blacksmith looks on, was once an everyday occurrence. **(Ben McKenzie collection)**

Packhorse Bells

Before the railway extensions, twenty years ago, Hawes was one of the most inaccessible places in the kingdom, being sixteen miles distant from the nearest station. The packhorse traffic lingered in this neighbourhood long after it had ceased in other parts of England. Handloom weaving was an old local industry, and when a sufficient number of pieces were ready, they were gathered up and conveyed by teams of pack-horses over the mountains to Settle, and thence by the road to Bradford and other West Riding towns. Discharging their loads they would return laden with warp, weft, size and other articles. Occasionally they crossed by the old Cam pass – a wild rough road in misty or wet weather – but their presence was generally known by the tinkling of the bells, which could be heard at a good distance, and at the head of the pass far down Langstrothdale. When the traffic ceased, hundreds of these sonorous pack-bells were sold for old metal, and the brokers' for a time were full of them. Each bell weighed from llb to 2lb.

Harry Speight, *Romantic Richmondshire*, 1897

Life in Upper Wharfedale in the 18th Century

Undoubtedly the greatest historian of the Dales, and a figure of national importance, DR THOMAS DUNHAM WHITAKER *(1759-1821) transformed topography into serious scholarship and enquiry. As a weakly and delicate boy, he was boarded out with a Reverend Sheepshanks in Grassington, and his first-hand knowledge of Dales life dates from this period, when he was a pupil at Threshfield Grammar School. He eventually became vicar of Whalley, Lancashire writing his fine* History of Whalley *before undertaking the remarkable* History of Craven *in 1805. The work remains to this day a model of careful scholarship and patient research, to which grateful scholars and topographers of succeeding generations have turned. Many of the more picturesque accounts of Craven history owe their origin to Whitaker's brilliant researches among documentary evidence.*

His transference to the industrial parish of Blackburn in 1818 proved too exhausting to the ailing scholar and his grandiose plans for a history of Yorkshire never materialized, the first volume being published with the celebrated engravings by Turner as the History of Richmondshire *in 1823.* Richmondshire *has nothing of the earlier work's insight and clarity.*

Another part of the subject which yet remains in the antiquated modes of life which prevailed till within the last eighty years among the yeomanry of Wharfedale. These may be illustrated by the manners of Linton in particular....

I suspect them to be of high antiquity; for though the race of independent yeomanry, the happiest, and probably the most virtuous condition of life in the kingdom, arose in Wharfedale, partly from the dispersions of the estates of the monasteries, and partly out of the vast alienations made by the Cliffords, yet, before either of those eras, the tenantry lived in so much plenty and security, the tenements descended so regularly from father to son, and the control exercised over them by their lords was of so mild a nature, that the transition from occupancy to property would not be marked by any violent change of

Threshfield Grammar School, where the famous Dales historian Thomas Whitaker was a pupil. He noted that 'the facilities of learning were great', young people of both sexes availing themselves of instruction which was considered 'a sort of carnival'
(Ben McKenzie collection)

Today's fare would no doubt seem sumptuous to dalesfolk of earlier times. Gregson and Nelly Porter of Throstle Nest, Gunnerside, are about to enjoy this traditional farmhouse tea - complete with all the trimmings - in 1985 (*Marie Hartley*)

manners of habits. But to be more particular.

There was a considerable quantity of hemp, and more anciently of line or flax, from which the place derives its name, grown within the township of Linton, which the inhabitants spun and prepared themselves. Almost every woman could spin flax from the distaff, or rock, as it was called, and card and spin wool from the fleece. There were no poor rates and no public houses. In 1740 every housekeeper in the township, excepting one, kept a cow. The estates were small, and the number of little freeholders considerable in proportion; almost all of these farmed their own property, and lived upon the produce.

At this time tea was scarcely introduced; for I remember a very sensible man, who declared that when he first saw the school-master drinking this beverage he could not conceive what refreshment he was taking.

Every landowner had a small flock of sheep, and fatted one or two hogs every winter. They all grew oats, which formed the principal article of their subsistence. The kiln, in which the grain was parched previously to its being ground, belonged to the township, and when in use was a sort of coffee-house, where the politics of the place and the day were discussed.

Their bread, and most of their puddings, were made of oatmeal; and this, mixed with milk, or water when milk was scarce, supplied them with breakfast and supper. Each owner, too, grew his own barley, and manufactured his own malt. The large steeping-trough, which belonged to the village in general, remained within my recollection. Very little fresh meat was eaten except at their annual feasts, when cattle were slaughtered and sold by persons who never exercised the trade at any other time. Indeed, under such a system of manners, there could scarcely be any tradesman; every man exercised, however imperfectly, almost every trade for himself. The quantity of money in circulation must have been inconceivably small. One great advantage of these simple habits was, that superfluous wealth and abject poverty were equally excluded....

Almost everything was in common. There was a stone called the batting stone, where the women of the place beat their linen with battledores after having rinsed it in the brook; a necessary process, partly out of the vast alienations made by the Cliffords, yet, before as it had previously been washed in a certain animal fluid, a very disgusting substitute for soap and water. Their linen was rarely smoothed with heated iron.

Their early hours rendered their consumption of candles excepting in the depths of winter, very trifling, and those were merely rushes partly peeled and dipped in coarse fat.

Cheeses were almost universally made at home; but as few kept a sufficient number of cows for this purpose, village partnerships were formed, and the milk of several farms thrown together in succession.

Few hired servants, male or female, were kept, but where this was done little distinction was kept up between the different members of the family; they invariably ate and worked together, the only effectual method to ensure diligence and prevent waste in dependents. The wages of labourers were very low, not exceeding twopence halfpenny a day with board. The facilities of learning were great. A grammar-school prepared many natives of the village for the University at no expense but part of their time. The price of a day-school was two shillings per quarter, and an excellent writingmaster attended for some weeks every year at the free school for sixpence a week per scholar. Young people of both sexes availed themselves of his instruction, and the time was considered a sort of carnival.

TDC Whitaker, *The History and Antiquities of the Deanery of Craven*, 1805

The Knitters of Dent

But perhaps the most characteristic custom of the Dales, is what is called their Sitting, or going-a-sitting. Knitting is a great practice in the dales. Men, women, and children, all knit. Formerly you might have met the waggoners knitting as they went along with their teams; but this is now rare; for the greater influx of visitors, and their wonder expressed at this and other practices, have made them rather ashamed of them, and shy of strangers observing them. But the men still knit a great deal in the houses; and the women knit incessantly. They have knitting schools, where the children are taught; and where they sing in chorus knitting songs, some of which appear as childish as the nursery songs of the last generation. Yet all of them bear some reference to their employment and mode of life; and the chorus, which maintains regularity of action and keeps up the attention, is of more importance than the words. Here is a specimen:

Bell-wether o' Barking,* cries baa, baa,
How many sheep have we lost today?
Nineteen we have lost, one have we faun'
Run Rockie†, run Rockie, run, run, run.

This is sung while they knit one round of the stocking; when the second round commences they begin again

Bell-wether o' Barking, cries baa, baa,
How many sheep have we lost today?
Eighteen we have lost, two have we faun'
Run Rockie, run Rockie, run, run, run.

and so on till they have knit twenty rounds, decreasing the numbers on the one hand, and increasing them on the other.

These songs are sung not only by the children in the schools, but also by the people at their sittings, which are social assemblies of the neighbourhood, not for eating and drinking, but merely for society. As soon as it becomes dark, and the usual business of the day is over, and the young children are put to bed, they rake or put out the fire; take their cloaks and lanterns, and set out with their

---

*a mountain overlooking Dent.
†the shepherd's dog.

knitting to the house of the neighbour, where the sitting falls in rotation, for it is a regularly circulating assembly from house to house through the particular neighbourhood. The whole troop of neighbours being collected, they sit and knit, singing knitting songs, and tell knitting-stories. Here all the old stories and traditions of the dale come up, and they often get so excited that they say "Neighbours, we'll not part tonight," that is, till after twelve o'clock. All this time their knitting goes on with unremitting speed. They sit, rocking to and fro like so many weird wizards. They burn no candle, but knit by the light of the peat fire. And this rocking motion is connected with a mode of knitting peculiar to the place, called swaving, which is difficult to describe. Ordinary knitting is performed by a variety of little motions, but this is a single uniform tossing motion of both hands at once, and the body accompanying it with a sort of sympathetic action. The knitting produced is just the same as by the ordinary method. They knit with crooked pins called pricks; and use a knitting-sheath consisting commonly of a hollow piece of wood, as large as the sheath of a dagger, curved to the side, and fixed in a belt called the cowband. The women of the north, in fact, often sport very curious knitting sheaths. We have seen a wisp of straw tied up pretty tightly, into which they stick their needles; and sometimes a bunch of quills of at least half-a-hundred in number. These sheaths and cowbands are often presents from their lovers to the young women. Upon the band there is a hook upon which the long end of the knitting is suspended that it may not dangle. In this manner they knit for the Kendal market, stockings, jackets, nightcaps, and a kind of cap worn by negroes, called bump-caps. These are made of very coarse worsted, and knit a yard in length, one half of which is turned into the other, before it has the appearance of a cap.

The smallness of their earnings may be inferred from the price for the knitting of one of these caps being threepence. But all knit, and knitting is not so much their sole labour as an auxiliary gain. The woman knits when her housework is done; the man when his out-of-doors work is done, as they walk about their garden, or go from one village to another, the process is going on. We saw a stout rosy girl driving some cows to the field. Without anything on her head, in her short bedgown and wooden clogs, she went on after them with a great stick in her hand. A lot of calves which were in the field seemed determined to rush out, but the damsel laid lustily about

Martha Dinsdale of Appersett, one of the last of the Dales handknitters. In the 1930s she was paid six shillings (30p) to knit six sailors' jerseys (*Bertram Unne*)

her with her cudgel, and made them decamp. As we observed her proceedings from a house opposite, and, amused at the contest between her and the calves, said, "well done! dairymaid!" "O" said the woman of the house, "that is no dairymaid; she is the farmer's only daughter, and will have quite a fortune. She is the best knitter in the dale." That is, the young lady of fortune, earned a shilling a day.

The neighbouring dale, Garsdale, which is a narrower and more secluded one than Dent, is a great knitting dale. The old men sit there in companies around the fire, and so intent are they on their occupation and stories, that they pin cloths on their shins to prevent them being burnt; and sometimes they may be seen on a bench at the housefront, and whence they have come out to cool themselves, sitting in a row knitting with their shin-cloths on, making the oddest appearance imaginable.

William Howitt, *The Rural Life of England*, 1844

The Wensleydale Knitters

Simplicity and industry characterize the manners and occupations of the various humble inhabitants of Wensley Dale. Their wants, it is true, are few; but to supply these, almost constant labour is required. In any business where the assistance of the hands is not necessary, they universally resort to knitting. Young and old, male and female, are all adepts in this art. Shepherds attending their flocks, men driving cattle, women going to market, are all thus industriously employed. A woman of the name of Slinger, who lived in Cotterdale, was accustomed regularly to walk to the market at Hawes, a distance of three miles, with the weekly knitting of herself and family packed in a bag upon her head, knitting all the way. She continued her knitting while she staid at Hawes, purchasing the little necessaries for her family, with the addition of worsted for the work of the ensuing week; all of which she placed upon her head, returning occupied with her kneedles as before. She was so expeditious and expert, that the produce of the day's labour was generally a complete pair of men's stockings.

George Walker, *The Costume of Yorkshire*, 1814

Wensleydale knitters - as depicted in *The Costume of Yorkshire* (1814)

Children of Oughtershaw School *(Bertram Unne)*

A Child of the Dales

From the classroom window rolled the great expanse of the Dale.
The sad child in the corner stared out like a rabbit in a trap,
'He has special needs,' explained the teacher, in a hushed, maternal voice,
'Real problems with his reading, and his number work is weak.
Spelling non-existent, writing poor, he rarely speaks.
He's one of the less able in the school.'

The lad could not describe the beauty that surrounded him,
The soft green dale and craggy hills.
He could not spell the names
Of those mysterious places which he knew so well.
But he could tickle a trout, ride a horse,
Repair a fence and dig a dyke,
Drive a tractor, plough a field,
Milk a cow and lamb a ewe,
Name a bird by a faded feather,
Smell the seasons and predict the weather.
Yes, that less able lad could to all those things.

Gervase Phinn, *The Other Side of the Dales,* 1998

The Dalesman

Herbert Bentham of Dockle Syke Farm, Deepdale, photographed in 1958. (*Geoffrey N. Wright*)

T C ('Kit') Calvert, creator of the modern Wensleydale cheese industry, who was often described as 'the complete dalesman'

The Dalesman has a deep and often partly concealed sense of humour, frequently with a grim turn or touched with something of the macabre, his quick wit in repartee has the same flavour. All this is a reflection of the age-old struggle against a tough environment in which living means constant effort. He is a hard bargainer and is careful, even 'near' in money matters, but again this is a product of making a living that is possible only by hard work and constant watchfulness amid conditions that often appear adverse. The true Dalesman has integrity and, like Wycliffe, holds his 'unswerving convictions', often mistakenly described as obstinacy by those who know him least well. Withal, he has generosity and a great impulse to hospitality. The qualities are blended with an intense local pride and love and loyalty to his dale, never flaunted but always there, a part of his nature.

Arthur Raistrick, *Open Fell, Hidden Dale,* 1985

Portrait of a daleswoman - Mrs B Simpson of Higher Platts Farm, Summerbridge, Nidderdale *(Bertram Unne)*

Industry in the Dales

The New Cotton Mill at Aysgarth

I descended to the Bridge of Asgarth; there sending back my horses to the public house, and ordering G. to return with a guide.

During his long absence, I had to admire the delicious scenery, around this charmingly-placed bridge; whose wildness has been sadly demolish'd by a late (adametic) reparation, and the cutting down of the ivy.

But what has completed the destruction of every rural thought, has been the erection of a cotton mill on one side, whereby prospect, and quiet, are destroy'd: I now speak as a tourist (as a policeman, a citizen, or a statesman, I enter not the field); the people indeed, are employ'd; but they are all abandon'd to vice from the throng.

If men can thus start into riches; or if riches from trade are too easily procured, woe to us men of middling income, and settled revenue; and woe it has been to all the Nappa Halls and the Yeomanry of the land.

At the times when people work not in the mill, they issue out to poaching, profligacy and plunder. Sr Rd. Arkwright may have introduced much wealth into his family, and into the country; but as a tourist, I execrate his schemes, which, having crept into every pastoral vale, have destroy'd the course, the beauty of Nature; why, here now is a great flaring mill, whose back stream has drawn off half the water of the falls above the bridge.

With the bell ringing, and the clamour of the mill, all the vale is disturb'd; treason and levelling systems are the discourse; and rebellion may be near at hand.

John Byng, *A Tour to the North*, 1792 (from *The Torrington Diaries*)

The Story of Malham Mill

It stood in one of the most romantic positions for which poet or novelist could ask. Only about a third of a mile from the magnificent Malham Cove, a limestone cliff 240ft high and about 350 yards across the chord of its splendid curve, the mill straddled as a bridge across the powerful stream which emerges at the foot of the cove after a long underground course. The stream plunges over a waterfall, at the foot of which the mill stood, almost within reach of its spray. The height of the fall and a slight dam across the stream gave plenty of head for the mill-wheel, and although only traces of the bridge foundations and of the dam and goit remain, it is not at all difficult to recreate the impressive picture the mill must have made when this gorge to the cove was better wooded than it is now.

In the opening years of the thirteenth century John Aleman gave his cornmill at Malham, with suit of 2s (10p) a year, to Fountains Abbey for the support of the poor folk who gathered at the abbey gate. In 1450 the bursar of the abbey valued it as £1, and at the Dissolution it was still one of the many mills owned and valued by the abbey. At the Dissolution it was bought with other Malham estates but continues to work as a cornmill. In 1680, when Thomas Atkinson had been the miller for eighteen years, a dispute over the dues to be paid by tenants of Malham

The 'old mill by the stream' - revered by countless writers down the ages - survived in the Dales until quite recently. Here is Beamsley Mill, near Bolton Abbey, looking very much part of the rural idyll about 1950

showed that, instead of a uniform rate for grinding corn, some tenements in the village paid one-twentieth and some one twenty-fourth, and these differences went back into past history.

Early in the eighteenth century it ceased to work as a cornmill, and in 1797 it had been converted to a cotton mill and was leased by its then owner, Brayshaw, to the three Cockshutt brothers. In 1815 it was re-leased for twenty-four years to the Cockshutts, along with John and Joseph Lister of Haworth, "cotton twist spinners", but a third part was subject to a mortgage taken by one of the brothers. The rent was £120 a year and the mill structure, the water-wheel and pit-wheel, upright shafts and naked

tumbling shafts, with the miller's house, dam, goit and other appurtenances, were to be insured against fire for £2,400. The machinery in the mill was valued at £564 and there were ancient water rents of 5s (25p) and 2s 6d (12$\frac{1}{2}$p) per year and a lord rent of 13s 33/4d (66$\frac{1}{2}$p). In this lease we glimpse something of the arrangement of the mill drive. The pitwheel would be a large-diameter gear-wheel driving through bevel wheels the vertical shaft on which the other bevel-wheels would turn the driving shaft, the tumbling shafts, on each floor of the mill. This lease, which was for twenty-four years, was renewed and for some time the mill continued to be worked by Cockshutts as a cotton mill, but ceased before 1847 when it was noted by the Ordnance Survey as a cotton mill in ruins. A few years later it was pulled down and the stone was used to build the Ploughleys Barn in Malham West Field. All that now remain are the name Old Mill Foss and slight traces of the bridge and goit.

Arthur Raistrick, *Old Yorkshire Dales*, 1967

The Craven Lead Miners

Miners in general, I might almost say universally, are a most tumultuous, sturdy people, greatly impatient of control, very insolent, and much void of common industry. Those employed in the lead mines of Craven, and in many collieries, can scarcely, by any means, be kept to the performance of a regular business; upon the least disgust, they quit their service, and try another. No bribes can tempt them to any other industry after the first performance of their work, which leaves them half a day for idleness, or rioting in the alehouse.

Arthur Young, *An Account of the present state of Agriculture, Manufacturers and Population in several counties of this Kingdom*, 1770

The Grassington Moor Mines

– Our mines produce several sorts of ore,
But chiefly lead, – we have it in great store
At Patley-bridge and Green-how-hill anon,
On Craven-Moor and likewise Grassington;
There may be seen brought from the earth to light,
Great heaps of lead ore shining and bright;
By horses, wheel and ropes, and tubs for drawing,
So deep they seem quite overawing;

Then they proceed to dress the beauteous ore,
By grateing, grinding, washing o'er and o'er;
Then to the furnace which by fire is fed
Which soon refines it into solid lead;

John Broughton, "On Craven" 1828 from *Poems: Moral, Sentimental and Satirical*

A Calamity

Excepting what always must be excepted, the introduction of manufactories, I do not know a greater calamity which can befall a village than the discovery of a lead-mine in the neighbourhood.
T.D. Whitaker, *History of Craven*, 1805

Harris Shaft dressing floor, Greenhow Hill. Boys often worked at the lead mines from ages as young as nine. The hats resembling deerstalkers had a serious purpose, the idea being to stop water from running down the back of the neck *(**Beamish North of England Open Air Museum**)*

A Tourist Trip to the Mines

No visitor to Grassington ought to omit a visit to the mines which are about two or three miles from the town. They commenced working them before the time of James the First, and it was stated at a public meeting held in Skipton, in connection with the Skipton and Wharfedale Railway, that even lately they produced a profit of ten thousand pounds per annum. It is very interesting to strangers to enter them, though perhaps the descent may frighten them a little. The bottom of some of the shafts are reached by ladders, and others by ropes. When you are safely down you will be led by one of the miners into the different "levels", holding in your hand a candle in a piece of clay, to keep your hand from melting the tallow by its warmth. At the first it will prove curious work for you, sometimes to be "climbing up ladders then rambling over rocks, then wading through water, then marching through mud, then creeping through holes; at times clambering up a narrow bore, hobbling along a narrow passage, squeezing through a tortuous crevice; then going on all fours, bear fashion, crawling, scrambling, struggling" along the subterranean recesses, from which the precious ore has been dug. But to see the rich veins of lead "glinting and sparkling like jewels in the rock", and the "little caverns of spar" – "glittering grottos of well-defined crystal" – that "sparkle like fairy halls", or "miniature palaces of pearl, spangled with more than oriental splendour", will give pleasure that will more than reward you for your toil.

Bailey J. Harker, *Rambles in Upper Wharfedale*, 1869

Old Gang lead smelting mill, between Swaledale and Arkengarthdale. At top left is the peat house, originally ling-thatched and designed to hold at least a year's supply of fuel *(Marie Hartley)*

A Visit to Arkengarthdale

12th September, 1817

Left Wensley with Mr Costabadie and Mr Maude for Arkendale, travelled over a moor entirely covered with ling to Reeth, a beautiful little town situated in Swale Dale and surrounded with mountains covered with ling, called on Mr Hall who has a fine collection of the produce of the Yorkshire Cumberland and Durham mines, did not see Mr H. but Mrs H. shewed us the collections, met there a Mr Harland a particularly handsome man who gave us a few specimens of carbonate of barytes with which the

Swale Dale and Arkendale mines particularly abound, brought also a few at a shop and a few at the inn. Proceeded from Reeth to Arkendale with a letter of introduction to a Mr Tilburn who seemed at first not to know what a mineral was, tho' he was a principal clerk in the lead works, however he found us a conductor who led us towards the mouth of the level which he said was about $1/2$ a mile further off on a very high ground which as it was near 3 o'clock was too laborious for us to attempt, we therefore returned to Mr Tilburn who gave us a few very good specimens and our guide having brought us also a few and having picked up a few from the miners living in the village of Arkendale we returned to Wensley tolerably well loaded and got there about $^1/_2$ past 7. The girls and H. Costabadie had ordered dinner before I arrived and had eaten part of it. Mrs C. and Mr Maude did not arrive till we had finished and Mr C was very angry at the young ones having gone to dinner before our return as Mr C. dined that day at Leyburn Book Club.

Rev. Benjamin Newton, *Journal*

The Settle and Carlisle Line

The railway from Settle to Carlisle is probably the most remarkable and interesting work of its kind in England remarkable for the engineering difficulties that have been overcome, and interesting in the scenery through which it passes. It had long been known that if a railway were ever carried in this direction, extraordinary obstacles would have to be surmounted. Over any such path to the North "frown the huge masses of Ingleborough and Whernside, and Wildboar and Shap Fells, and if a line were to wend its way at the feet of these, it would have to be by spanning valleys with stupendous viaducts and piercing mountain heights with enormous tunnels; miles upon miles of cuttings would have to be blasted through the rock, or literally torn through clay of the most remarkable tenacity, and embankments, each weighing perhaps 250,000 tons, would have to be piled on peaty moors, on some parts of which a horse could not walk without sinking up to his belly". Only one route was possible – along a chain of four deep valleys which in rough and massive outline stretched from south to north, the more southern rising up one of the wildest, windiest, coldest and drieriest parts of the world, and the more northern falling gently down one of the most beautiful districts in England – the Vale of the Eden. The engineer-in-chief has described the route of his line in homelier phraseology. He has said that the country may be compared to a great whale lying on its belly, with its nose at Settle and its tail at Carlisle. A steep ascent carries us up, a long incline carries us down.

Leaving the 'metropolitan town' of Settle, overlooked by the lofty limestone rock of Castleber, we start upon our journey up the noble valley of the Ribble, apparently closed in the north by the mighty outlines of Whernside and Pennegent, often hid in gloomy clouds of trailing mist. Passing the works of the Craven Lime Company, we reach Stainforth, and cross the roaring Ribble. About eight miles from Settle we are at the village of Selside, near which is Hellen Pot, which Mr. J. R. Thornson declares to be "the most awful thing in all England" – a terrific chasm, 60 feet wide and more than 300 deep, down which a waterfall leaps into the gloom. Four miles from Selside we cross the turnpike which runs from Ingleton to Hawes, and now the heaviest part of the work of the railway begins. Here, a few years since, not a vestige of a habitation could be seen, and the only signs of life were the grouse, and anon a black-faced mountain sheep, half buried among the ling. We are now approaching the great hill of Blea Moor, an outlying flank of the mighty Whernside, through which, at a height of 1,100 feet above the sea, the renowned Blea Moor tunnel had to be carried. Speaking of this spot, Mr. Allport says: "I shall not forget as long as I live the difficulties that surrounded us in that undertaking. Mr. Crossley and I went on a voyage of discovery – 'prospecting'. We walked miles and miles; in fact I think I may safely say we walked over a greater part of the line from Settle to Carlisle, and we found it comparatively easy sailing till we got to that terrible place, Blea Moor. We spent an afternoon there looking at it. We went miles

The 1,169ft summit of the Settle to Carlisle railway at Ais Gill, with Wild Boar Fell brooding in the background. A picture by the famous railway photographer, Bishop Eric Treacy, who was especially adept at depicting trains in the landscape

down which the Dee roars on part of its way – over a bed of black marble, skirted by the greenest of green meadows where herds of cattle pasture, while on either side rise the moorlands, the wildest and loneliest in Yorkshire.

without seeing an inhabitant, and the Blea Moor seemed effectually to bar our passage northward". We are now at Dent Head, and away to the north stretches the valley

The Official Guide to the Midland Railway, 1880

Ribblehead Viaduct
and
Blea Moor Tunnel

Having referred to the prominent natural features about Ribblehead, let us say a word about the most striking work of man to be seen here. This is the immense *railway viaduct* constructed by the Midland Railway Company for the passage of trains between Settle and Carlisle. It crosses Batty Moss, and gave the contractors some trouble before solid and durable foundations could be obtained. Nearly all the piers rest on a bed of concrete six feet thick, laid upon solid rock. The length of the viaduct is 1328 feet, composed of 24 arches of an average span of 45 feet, and the height of the loftiest from the parapet to the foundations is 165 feet. It contains 34,000 cubic yards of masonry, besides 6000 feet of concrete. About a mile to the north of it (between Ribblehead and Dent) is the famous Blea Moor tunnel, one of the longest in England, being 2460 yards in length and 500 feet below the outer surface at the deepest part. The metals in the tunnel attain an altitude of 1151 feet. Blea Moor and Wold Fell being on the watershed of England, the streams of the latter descending westward, drain into the Irish Sea, and eastward into the German Ocean.

Harry Speight, *Tramps and Drives in the Craven Highlands*, 1895

Ribblehead viaduct under construction in the early 1870s. A vast shanty town, known as Batty Wife Hole, sprang up to house some two thousand navvies who converged on this remote moorland setting

Railway Boom in Sedbergh

Thirty three years ago we were half a dozen miles from a railway station. Then the opening of the Ingleton and Tebay branch of the London and North Western Railway abridged the distance to a mile; and, last of all, competing omnibuses have achieved the irreducible minimum, and gently drop all who deign to visit us at our doors. The market has improved in consequence. From an applecart and half a dozen admiring nondescripts, it has grown to a fairly busy throng of buyers and sellers. Among other things we abound in butter, and connoisseurs in this commodity, from populous towns like Bradford, personally or by proxy, relieve us of the golden store. The School has developed enormously, and affectionate parents look in upon us from time to time. Land in suitable situations has been set aside for building plots, and comfortable residences of modern aspect are springing up apace. Multiplied wants have quickened industry and stimulated enterprise. Gas-works, waterworks, sewerage schemes, and all the resources of civilisation are upon us.

We are verily and indeed going ahead; and if the Rip Van Winkles who fell asleep half a century ago were permitted to walk this earth again, they would rub their

The opening of the railway from Ingleton to Tebay conferred huge benefits on Sedbergh - including its famous public school. Special trains conveying boys and their trunks ran at the beginning and end of each term. An era came to an end in September 1964, when one of the last two specials was photographed crossing Lune viaduct. The flanks of the Howgills are in the background (*Derek Cross*)

eyes with manifest astonishment. Summer visitors have found us out, and, with increased accommodation, will be here in great numbers. Even plethoric excursion trains, after disgorging the major part of the contents at Ingleton, bring forward adventurous spirits bent on extending their conquests over the realms of space who, after a few hours' experience of our wholesome upland air, carry back to dingy streets the refreshing memory of progressiveness before us; and to the prophetic eye, that time is not far distant when the rural restfulness and picturesque scenery of the dales and hills will be more widely known and valued.

Rev. W. Thompson, *An illustrated Guide to Sedbergh, Garsdale and Dent*, 1894

Havoc, Dirt and Smoke at Aysgarth Falls

OUIDA, *the pseudonym of the popular novelist Marie Louise de La Ramé (1839-1908), was stirred to produce this brilliant polemic in support of the Aysgarth Defence Association, a group of local landowners and conservationists, anxious to preserve the unspoiled beauties from the depradations of the railway engineers who proposed a railway line from Skipton to Aysgarth, meeting the existing North Eastern Railway line in the vicinity of Aysgarth Falls. Its significance lies not in its effect on the railway project (which was, in any event, financially unsound) but as perhaps the earliest demonstration of a national movement for the conservation of the Yorkshire Dales.*

The Editor
The Times
Sir,
The opponents of the projected extension of the Skipton and North Eastern Junction Railway to Aysgarth Force have written to me to ask for my public assistance in these columns. I should be happy indeed could I hope that any words of mine would have the power to stem the tide of ruin from contractors' heedless greed, which in devastating the whole world, and from which England, by reason of her small proportion and crowded soil, suffers the most hideously.

The opponents of this railway extension can prove that it has not the slightest excuse of any utility, as the farmers in this portion of the Yorkshire Dales are all of them already within a few miles of market towns for their cattle and produce, while the reckless brutality which would thus destroy one of Turner's best loved scenes cannot be too severely censored. I say "destroy" because not only would the contemplated railway works, which cross Aysgarth Falls in a high brick bridge raised on skew arches, annihilate all the beauty of these secluded waterfalls for ever, but the erection of the bridge and function of a junction would inevitably be accompanied by all the havoc, dirt and smoke, and general ruin of green and trees, of streams and atmosphere, which are the attendant Furies of every engineering works. A little while ago, contractors, who have neither eye nor ear, neither sentiment nor sense, for anything save the immediate opportunity of putting money in their own pockets, actually brought forward a scheme to make a railway through Dovedale, to poison the classic stream beloved of Izaak Walton, and to carry the vileness of steam, stench and soot into that lovely world of transparent waters, waving reeds, aquatic plants and wood-clothed cliffs, which still remains serene and fair as in the days of the gentle Father of Anglers. Of this more anon, if ever the iniquitous plan should be mooted again; as yet Dovedale has been saved. What is immediately menaced now, and what will be doomed unless the House of Commons will consent to save it, is Turner's Aysgarth of the High Force. A committee of Yorkshire gentlemen is already formed, and all who love nature and the memory of that great painter of it are entreated to send in their names to Mr John Henry Metcalf, Leyburn, Wenslydale, a Yorkshireman, who, as dalesman born and bred, is foremost in his efforts to save his noble country from this defilement and degradation. The falls of the Yore at Aysgarth united to the heather-clad fells and the flowing pastures and golden gorse and blossoming thyme around them, are foremost among which a nation should be most grateful for and should most completely protect. If the junction intended to be made there is made, 'Arry and his bestial associations will speedily replace the innocent loveliness which no hand of man's can ever again restore.

A railway may be said to be, at its best, a questionable advantage; it beggars as many as it benefits, it enlarges the take of a town at the cost of half-a-dozen others, whilst any utility it may offer is dearly purchased by the pollution of the air and the noxious gases it creates. If science has any of the wisdom it pretends to possess, so ugly, noisy, clumsy and dangerous a method of locomotion as railways offer will, before 50 years have passed, be superseded by some other invention. Meanwhile, why deface the country, spoil the air, and vulgarize solitudes that are the parents of all high thoughts, in the sole interest of railway contractors? The extraordinary apathy of English people before the wholesale destruction of the natural beauty of their country is in strange contrast with their affected wakening to the necessity for artistic beauty within their homes. The contrast would be ludicrous were it not so melancholy.

I remain Sir, obediently yours
OUIDA
Friday February 1st, 1884

The Stone Men

On guard in dusk's violet dome
    a young and cut-throat moon
    reflects the south-west sun
that floodlights, though gone early home,
    our mountain's ermine fin.

Over the valley – Dis,
    quarry and limeworks – wars
    with explosive on ancient moors.
Thence, like a travelling house,
    glides the low light-hollowed bus.

It pauses to take me in
    to its mobile sitting room:
    I pay for my journey and turn
expecting the usual din
    of the widows riding to town.

Instead, in silent pairs,
    like statues carved in stone,
    grey with lime, in the gloom,
on the bus's double chairs
    sit quarrymen, going home.

The sculptor's cast of thought
    was the social realist school:
    his patiently chipping tool
drew snapbags, peaked caps, short
    thick donkey-jackets, and all

these death-mask-plaster faces
    with stonedust powdered hair
    and darkness-seeing stare
of men who've spent their forces
    in Earth-subduing war.

For Earth wears all men out –
    even the mountain-movers
    and their globe-lifting levers;
so widows laugh about
    the prowess of dead lovers

while snow creeps down the hill,
    and buses, through cut drifts
    shuttle the changing shifts,
and new children, to school,
    down valleys quarry-cliffed.

Anna Adams, 1977

Quarrying in the Dales - in days long before Health & Safety and hard hats.   The scene is Skirethorns, near Threshfield in Wharfedale. As at Burtersett, the stone was originally worked by driving 'levels' into the hillside and bringing the rock out on primitive railway wagons *(Ben McKenzie collection)*

Life at the Burtersett Quarries

The quarries were owned by Richard Metcalfe (Dicky Bocketer) and Tom Metcalfe, and these two quarry owners employed about 50 workers each. Also there were at least another two strangers to the district, prospecting along the hillside in the hope of finding a suitable seam of good slate and flagstones. These quarries were worked as "levels" running deep into the hillside, and the stone was dragged out by horse and bogie on a narrow gauge railway line.

Both quarry owners had two large waggons (four wheels) drawn by two horses to each waggon, which carried about 5 to 6 tons of dressed stone on each load, to Hawes Station, and was expected to deliver four load one and three load the next.

On the three load day the waggoner delivered three loads and loaded the fourth, bringing it to Burtersett, where it was left overnight loaded, so between them these four waggoners would deliver to the station approximately 80 tons of stone in various shapes and sizes each day.

This was when business was good, but it fluctuated enormously. Markets rose and fell in a depression, the quarrymen dressed stones in anticipation of better days, and the owners hoped for a break for the better. (Often they had to lay off men.)

By the time I was born (1903), "Dicky Bocketer" had twice been in financial difficulty, and "Tom Mecca" once, but they were still at the head of the businesses.

Dicky had built nine cottages in two rows on the east

side of the main street and Tom Mecca on the west side, facing each other. These were all occupied by quarrymen, and all other cottages were tenanted by quarrymen, but as about 100 men were employed many had to travel from Gayle, Hawes, Sedbusk and even Hardrow. In those days the railway bridge spanned the river, and Sedbusk workmen crossed over the bridge to get to and from work.

The top wage for a skilled worker either underground or on "The Hill" was 18/- (90p) per week for a six day week starting at 7.30 until 4pm – half an hour break for dinner. Many received 16/- (80p). "Sally Will Dick", a simple, honest workman, walked a distance of 3½ miles to and from Hardrow every day, a distance of 3½ miles single journey, and never had more than 16/- per week in his working life. Chipping wheelers started at 6/- a week and graduated to be craftsmen.

My Grandfather came from Gayle with his bride into one of the quarry owners' houses in the 1870s, worked for 18/- until age made him slower and his wage was reduced to 16/-, then he finally was turned off, to eke out a pittance working for the District Council, breaking stones at 1/10d (9p) per cubic yard, from Burtersett Lane bottom to the quarry gate (through Burtersett village) for £3 per annum.

T. C. 'Kit' Calvert, *Burtersett Seventy Years Ago*, 1974

Tan Hill
The last working coal mine in Swaledale

A mile down the road is the entrance to the Tan Hill coal mine, the largest and most important of the numerous pits which dot the moor around Tan Hill, others being King's Pit, Kettle Pot, the William Gill, and a small pit on the west slope of Shunner Fell. Their story, like that of the lead mines, is one of decline; Tan Hill is the last one (1934) to be working, and only two men are employed there.

It is not known when coal was first found on these moors, but in 1296 12d. was returned as a profit from a mine here, and in the fourteenth century a pit named Tackan Tarn was leased for 4 marks a year. Some years since a wooden pick tipped with iron was found in the mine, a relic of the days when iron was used sparingly. The last manager had in his possession an indenture made in 1670 between Phillip Lord Wharton and three men to whom he leased the mine. The agreement allowed Lord Wharton to take coal free of charge up to a hundred and fifty loads a year for use in his residence, Wharton Hall, Westmorland. At that time, Tan Hill and the smaller mines supplied coal to Swaledale, Wensleydale, Arkengarthdale, and Westmorland, and many men were employed. The coal was carried on pack-horses and donkeys; later, as the roads improved, carts were used. For farmers from the lower valleys the journey took two days; they would load their carts with produce from their farms and sell it on their way. There are men still living who can remember seeing processions of thirty or more carts when they arrived at their work at six o'clock in the morning. The coming of the railway to Hawes and Kirkby Stephen was the first step in the decline. Now motor lorries will deliver what they call 'station' coal anywhere, and the demand for 'pit' coal, which is harder and dirtier, grows less every year. But this hard coal is more economical than the 'station' coal, and it burns well with peat.

A track leads past the tumbling buildings to the level. This was started about ninety years ago and runs over a mile into the hill; it has always been hampered by water draining in from earlier workings. It is a friendly pit, and,

Tan Hill colliery, revived in the 1920s but in terminal decline a decade later. Long processions of carts once conveyed coal from here to Wensleydale, Swaledale and Westmorland *(Marie Hartley collection)*

though this may seem a contradiction, a country thing, part of the life of dalespeople, many of whom have worked there at some time. Surely no coal-mine ever spoilt its surrounding less. Hidden in a hollow, one must close upon it to see it. and even then it is possible to pass and not realise what it is. Already the moor has taken to herself again the tippings which it once turned out. It has its failings. Sometimes the roof of the level will slowly sink and shut the miners in at the far end. There they have to wait until their absence is discovered, and rescuers draw them up through a convenient shaft. One man coming with a load to the entrance saw the roof begin to sag, and bending low, dragged himself and the pony through just in time.

Ella Pontefract, *Swaledale* 1934

Visitors

No Use or Advantage to Man or Beast

Here, among the mountains, our curiosity was frequently moved to enquire what high hill this was, or that; and we soon were saluted with that old verse which I remembered to have seen in Mr Camden,

Ingleborough, Pendle Hill and Penigent
Are the highest hills between Scotland and Trent.

Indeed, they were, in my thoughts, monstrous high; but in a country all mountainous and full of innumerable high hills, it was not easy to judge which was the highest. Nor were these hills high and formidable only, but they had a kind of inhospitable terror in them. Here were no rich and pleasant valleys between them, as among the Alps; no lead mines and veins of rich oar as in the peak; no coal pits, as in the hills about Hallifax, much less gold as in the Andes, but all barren and wild, of no use or advantage to either man or beast....

Daniel Defoe, *A Tour Through the Whole Island of Great Britain* 1726

The Discomforts of the Drovers Inn

COLONEL JOHN BYNG (1743-1813) *a former Lieutenant-Colonel in the Guards Regiment who saw extensive service overseas, became a Civil Servant with the Inland Revenue before inheriting the title of the fifth Lord Torrington just a few months before his death. He undertook a number of remarkable journeys through England in the late eighteenth century, between 1781 and 1794.*

The journals he kept were not published until many years after his death, and provide a unique record of life in provincial England.

His account of the journey through the Yorkshire Dales in June 1792 from Teesdale to Swaledale, Askrigg, Hawes, Gearstones, Ingleton, Settle, Skipton and Malham is remarkable for the accuracy of its observation, its trenchant humour and the vitality of its author's style.

The ascent of the Mountain Cams is one of the longest, steepest, and most stoney in Great Britain; for they say it is 9 miles to the summit; the 1st 4 are very steep. If the roads are bad, the country barren, and the winters long, yet the inhabitants are compensated by the plenty of coal, the trout fishing, and the grouse shooting; which is a season ardently wish'd for; and brings a short harvest to the small inns. Upon the hillside we were encounter'd by some sharp stones....

I was much fatigued by the tediousness of the road-whereupon we at last met two farming men, with whom we conversed about the grouse, and their abundance. Crossing a ford, Mr Blakey led me to a public house – call'd Grierstones, the seat of misery, in a desert; and tho' filled with company, yet the Scotch fair upon the heath added to the horror of the curious scenery; the ground in front crowded by Scotch cattle and the drovers; and the house cramm'd by the buyers and sellers, most of whom were in plaids, fillibegs, etc. The stable did not afford hay. My friend, who knew the house, forced his way thro' the lower floor, and interned himself in the only wainscotted bedroom up stairs, where we at length we procured some boil'd slices of stale pork, and some fry'd eggs; with some wretched beer and brandy – to which my hunger was not equal; and from which my delicacy revolted. When our room was invaded by companions he

Thornton Force in the heart of the Three Peaks. This area was sought out by many early visitors to the Dales, even though accommodation was likened to 'the seat of misery in a desert' *(Dan Binns)*

call'd out—This is a private chamber."

The only custom of this hotel, or rather hovel, is derived from grouse shooters, or from two Scotch Fairs; when at the conclusion of the days of squabble, the two Nations agree in mutual drunkenness, the Scotch are allways wrap'd up in their plaids-as a defence against heat, cold or wet; but they are preventions of speed or activity; so wherever any cattle stray'd they instantly threw down the plaid, that they might overtake them. All Yorkshire around, tho' black, and frightful, seem of small account in the comparison of Ingleborough-at whose base we now travel. Mr Blakey's dog who was my only diversion on the road, seems thoroughly master of his business and worth 4 times the sum (3 guineas) that Mr B. gave for him. I believe he could sell him for 5 guineas. The reckoning being paid, very genteely, by me, I proposed to Mr. Blakey to ride forward to accelerate our intention.

There fell many storms of rain; and these come upon you in a mist, from the mountains, without giving the least warning. Our poor horses were glad to be delivered from their stye; and I then pursued Mr. Blakey's steps to a vale, call'd Chapel-in-dale; where, from the first house, he call'd to me. This was the habitation of a jolly shoemaker, a fine bold-looking fellow; and his wife, to whom he had not long been married, was an excellent contrast of sweet expression and feminine softness: he is the guide to the neighbouring caves, the noblest of which, Wethercote, is adjoining to his house, and presented us with ale in a *Silver cup*!! Perhaps there is no corner of this island that can afford wilder scenery; but Jobson thinks it is paradise: (and the winters roar but bind him to his native valley more.)

There is a horrid chas'm, just below his house, call'd Gingle-pot; down which we peep'd, and threw stones. But how shall I describe the wonders of Wethercote-Cave (Cove pronounced)?

From the top of this perpendicular cave are to be seen the falls of water that lose themselves at the bottom; and to which we approach'd by a most laborious descent; here two cascades are to be seen thro', upon a small passage leading into a horizontal cave: much wetting is to be encountered, and some danger apprehended. These cascades fall with an horrid din, filling the mind with a gloom of horror.

Honest Jobson now assured us that — "He must guide us to Yordas Cave-which was near at hand, and highly worth seeing"; but from the cold and frequent wettings, my curiosity was quell'd: however, Jobson insisted, and

Mr B. appeared anxious to see it.

So off we set; passing the small chapel, and some neighbouring houses, where Jobson bought a pound of candles, to carry with him to be lighted at the cave, from the burning turf he took in his hands. Our guide was a merry, hearty, fellow, and with much fun defended his County from our abuse, while we were crossing the terrible, stoney, mountain call's Gragareth – tho' he call'd it a short step, and strided away, (often renewing his fire with fresh peat,) where from bog, and stone, our horses could not keep pace with him, yet it appear's to me a distance of three miles.

Crossing a nasty, stoney brook, we arrived at Yordas Cave; where leaving our horses at the entrance, and lighting our candles we enter'd the cavern: it is well worthy of inspection, not too tedious, and beautifully closed by a cascade. Jobson stuck up candles by the way, which gave a most fanciful effect.

John Byng, *A Tour to the North*, 1792
(from *The Torrington Diaries*)

The Challenge of a Mountain

Though a stranger, and without a guide, I soon determined to try my strength in treading on the sides and summit of this noble mountain. I left my horse at a cottage, and in my ascent was surprised to find, that while many of the fertile plains of England were withering under the long-continued drought, the lower slopes of Ingleborough were luxuriant with verdure, and even afforded spoils for the scythe. In my ascent I disturbed many a homely couple of moor-game, who, in return, loudly scolded me for the intrusion, and hurried indignantly out of my sight; their rage was like the scolding of hens, but far louder.

I now came to my difficulties, and, as a child learning to walk, and afraid of falling, creeps on his hands and knees, then, to gratify my ambition, I crawled among the rocks fallen from the summit of the mountain. I durst not look behind me, lest my head should become giddy, so with alternate glimpses to what was above me, I looked right down to the earth; consequently my prospect extended but a few yards.

When I had nearly arrived at the top, I fell into a path, which, if I had entered at the beginning, my ascent would have been comparatively easy. I now stood on a plain, and I walked without apprehension. Two respectable persons that I joined, told me I had come up the worst way. Ingleborough may be said to take precedence of all the Yorkshire mountains: it stands prominent before the rest, and forms on its summit a spacious plain (said to be a mile in circumference), whereon might almost stand the adult population of the county. I should not have any objection to see it so assembled; but not to hold races, as I have been informed was sometimes the case. What would please me better, would be to see the population of Yorkshire so assembled around their late representative Wilberforce, and him on horseback addressing the multitude.

... Sunshine and shade furnished the beauties of contrast. The sun shining on a full sea from Lancaster to Millthorp and Ulverston appeared to spread as a plain, or rather to form a swell of glittering silver. The towers of Lancaster Castle, and its adjoining steeple, rose venerably in the distance. Clustering villages and white cottages, amid green fields and yellow harvests, spoke of peace and comfort to the admiring beholder.

In the Yorkshire part of the landscape was a peculiar trait. Far below where I stood at another season of the year, would have appeared considerable districts of snow; indeed they now, when the sun shone, seemed to glitter like fields of ice, and they literally appeared to be divided like fields in the landscape. The fact is, a species of white rock spreads over many scores of acres in this neighbourhood, and rises so little above the earth, and is so uniform on its surface, that a stranger might be so deceived as to pronounce it snow, ice, or fields spread with lime. I now looked over a limestone country a great distance, and the thought occured to me, that if all that ingredient in the composition of the earth now beneath my survey were to be burned into lime, it would furnish that article for the whole world for many ages.

Thomas Wilkinson, *Tours to the British Mountains*, 1824

Crossing the stepping stones at Bolton Abbey. A similar scene is likely to have greeted the Bronte family when they 'strolled through the grounds .. drinking in pleasure'. *(Ben McKenzie collection)*

An Excursion with the Brontes to Bolton Abbey

Ellen Nussey, a close friend of Charlotte Brontë, describes a visit made by the Brontë family in September 1833 to Bolton Abbey, a comfortable day out from Haworth in the days before railways.

It was I believe at the close of this visit that there was a clubbing together of pocket-money to secure an excursion to Bolton Abbey. Branwell Brontë undertook to procure a conveyance at a cheap rate which would carry <u>all</u> the party, and which, including the driver, would be six in number. The daily anticipation of the coming treat, mixed with apprehensions about the weather, was a perfect excitement to all.

Branwell seemed to know every inch of the way, could tell the names of the hills that would be driven over, their

exact height above the sea, the views to be seen, and the places to be passed through; it was an event to 'each' that, they were about to cross part of the range of hills which are designated the Back-bone of England.

The party started from the parsonage between five and six in the morning in a small double-gig or phaeton – it was partly a loan as well as a hire to Branwell. They were to meet friends and relatives who were to take Charlotte's friend home. The Haworth party chanced to drive up to the Hotel just before them, but in plenty of time to note,

Charlotte Bronte's little-known drawing of Bolton Abbey, with Bolton Bridge and Beamsley Beacon in the background. It was completed following a 'clubbing together of pocket money', which enabled the three Bronte sisters and their brother Branwell to make an excursion to Wharfedale in 1833 (*The Bronte Society*)

---

and go through what to 'their' young and enthusiastic hearts was 'quite' a new experience, (ie) that their <u>crowded</u> and <u>shabby-looking</u> conveyance 'which had been of no import whatever till now' was regarded with disdain by the hotel attendants, till they saw that they were cordially recognised by the handsome carriage-and-pair arrivals; all 'the party' breakfasted, and 'then' started on their stroll through the grounds.......

Emily and Anne hardly spoke during the whole excursion except to each other but it was easy to see how they were drinking 'in' pleasure and treasuring up the scenery in their minds. Charlotte who was acquainted with all the party, was less shy. Branwell who probably never knew the feeling of shyness, amused every one; he was in a phrensy of pleasure, his eyes flashed with excitement, and he talked fast and brilliantly; a friend who was present and herself a great admirer of scenery 'was much amused by his ecstasies' said she had never passed such a day of enjoyment in her life – She thought Branwell very eccentric, but recognised his rare talent and genius, she presaged though, the <u>danger of</u> those flashing impulses, a danger which cane so sorely and surely in after time. He had any amount of poetry ready for quotation, and this day he was well off in an appreciative audience whenever he chose to recite; it was one of the things he did well.

from *The Letters of Charlotte Brontë with a selection of letters by family and friends*, edited by Margaret Smith, 1995

The Toiling Artisans can reach the Dales

With Craven commences that romantic series of Dales which characterize the greater part of the North of England, and include within their precincts, not only that paradise of scenery, the Lakes, but many less known though scarcely less interesting 'localities; and now, not only the man of leisure and wealth, but the imprisoned denizen of the crowded town, and the toiling artizan will be enabled to visit these attractive places, for the newly constructed railways, though they may encroach a little upon the retirement and pastoral character of the country, offer a facility of transit, which even the pedestrian is sometimes glad to avail himself of, and a cheapness and speed of which the poor in money or in time may reap the benefit.

William Howson, *Illustrated Guide to the District of Craven*, 1850

Ask for Isabella

The Abbey of Fors took its name from the beautiful little waterfall of "fors" visible on your right just under Colby Hill. Going past Askrigg Mill, occupied by Mr. Addison, who is well "up" in the local history and in communicating his knowledge, cross a stone footbridge, and keep to the footpath till you reach nearly the top of the hill; then pass along a cart-road into the gill of Mill-Beck, and so on to the foot of *Mill Gill Fors*, a charming broken waterfall 69 feet high. Returning to the gate through which you entered, either follow the edge of the glen for a mile, where you will come to the top of *Whit-fell Gill Fors*, or, if you call at Mrs Little's at Helm, you may (if it is not Monday, her washing day), perhaps prevail upon her to allow her clever little "help" Isabella Scarr, to guide you by a rather difficult track to the foot of the fall. Seen either from above or below *Whit-fell Gill Fors* is "beautiful exceedingly" coming down in one unbroken sheet of water forty feet high.

George Hardcastle, *Wanderings in Wensleydale Yorkshire*, 1864

Whit-fell Gill Fors (now known as Whitfield Gill Force), as depicted in a painting attributed to Francis Nicholson (*Tennants Auctioneers*)

Dressed for the country? - a photo taken in Bolton Abbey Woods about 1895. Writers of the time often criticised ladies' outdoor apparel, commenting on the 'preposterous form of petticoat' and referring to women 'hooped with steel'

A Warning to Ladies

I should advise all persons who pilgrimate the valley, if it is but for a day, to take with them an extra pair of shoes and stockings; for whether they visit fall or fell, they are pretty sure to get wetshod in seeking the best points of view. Besides, by wading a beck here and there, one avoids many a long and weary detour; and no harm follows being wetshod if you only change your foot-gear as soon as your march is done. The walking tourist will find it very convenient to have his light marching-kit sent by the Mail-cart that goes up and down the valley every day, and calls at the principal villages on the route.

Females pilgrimating Wensleydale, on foot, will not "merrily hent the stile-a" so long as the present preposterous form of petticoat prevails. A distinguished foreigner remarks: "It is ridiculous to call woman's the softer sect when they are hooped with steel, and it is visible to the naked eye that are a deal more sterner than men's". The stiles of Wensleydale are narrow slits in the walls, on the average from six to eight inches wide; and some I saw measured only four inches.

George Hardcastle, *Wanderings in Wensleydale*, 1864

The First Descent of Alum Pot

PROFESSOR BOYD DAWKINS's *classic account of caves and caving belongs to a later epoch than other accounts of discovering the Dales. But his account of the first descent of Alum Pot is not another tourist tale; it captures the mixture of bravado and improvisation which made the early descents of the great potholes of Craven exploration on the heroic scale.*

The Helln Pot, into which the stream flowing through the Long Churn Cave falls, is a fissure a hundred feet long by thirty feet wide, that engulfs the waters of a little stream on the surface, which are dissipated in spray long before they reach the bottom. From the top you look down on a series of ledges, green with ferns and mosses, and, about a hundred feet from the surface, an enormous fragment of rock forms a natural bridge across the chasm from one ledge to another. A little above this is the debouchement of the stream flowing through Long Churn Cave through which Mr. Birkbeck and Mr. Metcalfe made the first perilous descent in 1847.

The party, consisting of ten persons, ventured into this awful chasm with no other apparatus than ropes, planks, a turn-tree, and a fire-escape belt. On emerging from the Long Churn Cave they stood on a ledge of rock about twelve feet wide, and which gave them free access to the "bridge". This was a rock about twelve feet wide, which rested obliquely on the ledges. Having crossed over this, they crept behind the waterfall which descended from the top, and fixed their pulley, five being let down while the rest of the party remained behind to hoist them up again. In this way they reached the bottom of the pot, which had never been trod by the feet of man. Thence they followed the stream downwards as far as the first great waterfall, down which Mr. Metcalfe was venturous enough to let himself with a rope, and to push onwards until daylight failed. He was within a very little of arriving at the end of the cave into which the stream flows, but was obliged to turn back into the daylight without having accomplished his purpose. The whole party eventually, after considerable danger and trouble, returned safely from the bold adventure.

J. Boyd Dawkins, *Cave Hunting*, 1874

Alum Pot, Ribblesdale, which pioneer cavers descended in heroic fashion using such primitive equipment as ropes, planks and fire escape belts

The Advantages of Railway Connection

HARDROW SCAR, HAWES,
NORTH YORKSHIRE.

The Committee have pleasure in announcing to the Public that (by the kind permission of the Right Honourable the Earl of Wharncliffe) they have made arrangements for holding their FIFTH ANNUAL

BRASS BAND & GLEE
CONTEST
AND
GRAND GALA
In Hardrow Scar Grounds,
On SATURDAY, JUNE 27TH, 1885,
WHEN PRIZES TO THE VALUE OF

£42   AND   £17
FOR BRASS BANDS   FOR GLEE SINGING
WILL BE OFFERED FOR COMPETITION.

AT THE CLOSE OF THE CONTEST, AN EFFICIENT QUADRILLE BAND WILL PLAY FOR

☞ **DANCING** ☜

WHICH WILL BE CONTINUED UNTIL ......

In Hardrow Scar Grounds there is a

MAGNIFICENT WATERFALL
Situate at the extremity of a deep, narrow, rocky Glen, along which the stream winds amongst detached masses of rock: an immense Column of Water ONE HUNDRED FEET HIGH being projected from the edge of a rock so as to detach itself completely from the strata beneath, and plunge without dispersion or interruption into a black and boiling caldron below. The Cataract is thrown forward in such a manner that a good carriage road might be made behind the Fall, in consequence of the action of the air having decomposed the shale underlying the grit and limestone. The Grounds are laid out with extensive walks, and contain several other beautiful Cascades.

EXCURSION TRAINS
Will run from LEEDS, BRADFORD, COLNE and CARLISLE on the Midland Railway, and EAST and WEST HARTLEPOOL, SOUTH BANK, MIDDLESBOROUGH, NORTH STOCKTON and DARLINGTON on the North Eastern Railway, calling at Intermediate Stations. For times of starting &c. see Railway Companies' Bills.

ADMISSION: ONE SHILLING EACH.
REFRESHMENTS WILL BE PROVIDED ON THE GROUND.
C. H. RICHARDSON Esq. President. J. W. FRYER Esq. Treasurer; EDWARD MOORE, Secretary

PRINTED BY THOS HESLOP, WENSLEYDALE PRINTING WORKS, HAWES.

Railway connection to Hawes fostered the famous 'Brass Band and Glee Contest' at Hardraw Scar. This poster of 1885 noted that excursion trains would run from such diverse points as Leeds, Bradford, Colne, Carlisle, West Hartlepool, Middlesbrough and Darlington

Some time ago now it was no uncommon thing to hear in Hawes (from persons who had at least fifty summers and who were in favour of travelling with the old stage coach and paying ls carriage on a letter) to say that it was a pity to see green fields cut up for a railway, and to argue with all the potinency of their natures that there is nothing like an old-fashioned warp after all. Since the introduction of railways into our neighbourhood, we have had the advantage never possessed by former generations. Now we have London newspapers, if we choose, delivered on the same day of issue. Now we have two deliveries of letters per day, viz at 9.30am and 6pm, an advantage which is highly appreciated by the inhabitants of Hawes. For the second delivery we are greatly, if not altogether indebted to our able postmaster, Mr E. Blythe, whose efforts to serve his fellow townsmen are untiring and unceasing. Now we have our merchandises brought to our doors at considerably less cost, and with half the delay, and what is prized by all, both rich and poor, we have coals at the station yard, at from $6\frac{1}{2}$d per cwt, good household coals. Who, we ask, would like to return to the old fashioned way of carting them (coals) 16 miles or more? Then, again, what a saving is effected by private individuals wishing to visit their friends living in any of the large towns, or tradespeople who have periodically to visit the markets at Manchester, Liverpool or London; who had to suffer the inclemency of the weather for 16 or 17 miles over wild moors and unsheltered roads, paying 16s or 21s for such a ride as the old fashioned ways afforded. Now they can travel, as it is needless to say, for infinitely less money and with incomparable comfort. Such are the advantages we in Hawes are deriving from railway connections; who would like to go back to the old times; or who would be grieved at running the iron road through the beautiful green fields of Wensleydale?

Craven Herald and Pioneer, 12th October, 1878

Midland Railway Pullman Cars, which in 1878 were the 'latest product of refined civilisation' for travellers on the Settle to Carlisle railway. What price today for similar standards of comfort on regular services over the line? (*National Railway Museum*)

The Dales in Armchair Comfort

Of all modes of travelling on wheels, there is one pre-eminent in luxurious comfort. Need we say that we refer to a journey in a Pullman Car on a Midland express? Availing ourselves of this latest product of refined civilisation, we took our places in the palace car which is attached to the Scotch express, on a bright and breezy day at the end of July. We were bound for the Craven country, and for the wild moorland mountainous region which has just been opened up for travellers and tourists by the new line from Settle to Carlisle. Seated on crimson velvet-piled armchairs, which, being fixed upon a pivot, admit of a semi-revolution, and surrounded by maps, guides and timetables, we prepared to enjoy the varied scenery through which we were to be driven by a powerful engine at high speed, and yet with the utmost possible speed and comfort.

J. Radford Thomson, *Guide to the District of Craven and the Settle and Carlisle Railway*, 1878

An Excursion Party to Ingleborough Cave

On arrival at Clapham Station, and luncheon at the Flying Horse Shoe Hotel directly opposite, carriages were brought into requisition, and the party driven to the pretty village of Clapham, which lies at the foot of Ingleborough Park, the residence of the Rev. T. M. Farrer, who is Lord of the Manor and principal landowner of the district. Mr Farrer was good enough to allow the Tourists to walk through his beautiful grounds to the entrance to the cave, which runs into the bowels of the lower Ingleborough range, for a distance of more than half a mile. These grounds are delightful and add greatly to the interest of this remarkable locality. The dell or gorge by which the cave is approached, runs into the hills between Ingleton and Settle, the upper part commencing in a precipitous scar, which bars the way, the limestone cliffs on all sides closing in a dell. A small stream issues from the scar, and joins lower down that flowing from the cave, which shortly forms the grand lake in the grounds under the hill. The narrow dell, the wooded heights, the rushing stream and occasional waterfall, were full of beauty, and the walk

Opposite Carriages were for long a standard means of conveyance in the Dales, as instanced by this magnificent scene of a coach-and-four at what is now the Devonshire Fell Hotel, Burnsall *(Alan Stockdale collection)*

Above Horses gradually gave way to motorised transport. Chapman's omnibuses operated a coach and mail service between Skipton and Buckden via Grassington, where one of their vehicles is posed outside the Temperance Hotel (now Church House) *(Ben McKenzie collection)*

along the terrace above the lake, to the cave, is sheltered and ornamented by the tender and graceful foliage of innumerable shrubs and trees. On reaching the entrance to the cave, the guide is first found, with candles ready lit for the tourists, in order to penetrate its dark recesses. A fairly defined road has been traced along the margin of the stream, which has frequently to be crossed, as the various cavities and chambers are reached. In some of the passages, stooping is requisite when the roof is low but they are frequently the vestibules to spacious and lofty chambers.

Ingleborough Cave is remarkable for the number and beauty of its stalactites and stalagmites some of which are quite transparent, whilst others are sonorous, and can

be made to imitate a peal of bells. Amongst the most marked are the Jockey's Cap, the Elephant's Legs, the Beehive, the Fleece and the Shower Bath. There are also many others bearing resemblance to natural objects or grotesque figures of animals and birds. The Gothic arch and pillared chamber are also prominent and particular features of this interesting cave. The cave, which is the largest in Yorkshire, has been penetrated to the extent of 1,000 yards, and the stream that runs through it finds its way from the slopes of Ingleborough through a deep chasm known as Gaping Gill.

J. Brown, *Tourist Rambles in the Northern and Midland Counties*, 1885

A picture postcard sent from Hebden in 1936 epitomising the gusto of the pre-war hiking movement. One group is taking enormous strides across the stepping stones and another is marching over the suspension bridge. Rucksacks and shorts are very much in evidence *(**Alan Stockdale collection**)*

The Hiking Craze

For years men have been tramping the hills and dales in increasing numbers and nobody took the least notice of them; but during the past year the noble legion of walkers became so formidable that obviously something had to be done about it.

And then, in some mysterious fashion, the old Saxon word "hiking" arrived on the American boat – and legs came into their own again! Perfectly respectable men who had never committed a crime in their lives, or done anything more sensational than climb Ingleboro', found their photographs confronting them in the newspapers on Monday morning in their old weather-beaten walking-

kit; more remarkable still, they found themselves as hikers in hiking bent! Useless for them to protest that they were no such thing, or that they had been tramping in the same kit long before the war. The mysterious power that shapes our ends and snaps us unawares decided that they were exponents of a new craze. Jokes began to be made about them. They were even said to be "iking" in every limb, which was clearly libellous. But very soon their novelty passed and the female hiker was discovered. At first she was recognisable as a genuine girl-walker in sensible skirt or shorts; but when this type palled, we were entertained to groups of reclining bathing belles who had obviously never walked further than the beach before. These, however, were "hikers" (or so it appeared) enjoying a temporary relaxation from the rigours of the Road. Even motorists picnicking by the roadside were photographed in all their glory and shown to belong to the true hiking breed.

Old hard-bitten ramblers laughed at the excellent jest and went on tramping and climbing as they had done before, until the temper of the reporters changed and they found themselves praised and photographed in one column as hikers and pilloried in the next for faults they had never committed: such as leaving litter and empty bottles on public commons, outraging decency, playing ukuleles and gramophones in peaceful glades, and generally behaving like hogs.

Is it surprising that the walker at last turned? In the West Riding, among the walking clubs and federations, the word "hike" is anathema, and press photographers are politely refused a special sitting.

Nevertheless, having said so much against it, let me admit that there is something to be said for the odious word "hike". It has drawn attention to the rapidly growing army of walkers, and the consequent publicity has helped to swell the ranks still more. Not all the recruits will last the pace; some are obviously attracted more by the possibilities for garish costume rather than from any real love for the road. Weird tribal head-dresses and brilliant blazers have appeared, and some of the ladies have cast convention to the winds and are returning to nature in too big a hurry. Many of these have not learnt the rudiments of the art and craft of tramping. They wander in pathetic clusters along arterial roads, singing sentimental songs, and looking tired to death before the day is half spent. Even so, I would not be thought for a moment to sneer at them. On the contrary I welcome them with open arms. Many of them, no doubt, will soon tire of the road and find solace or sensation in gliding or football instead, for the modern girl is nothing if not versatile. But a large number of them will get over their growing pains and develop into real ramblers and trampers in time. And there

are thousands of others – girls and youths – who have taken to walking in earnest during the last two years, as the new clubs and journals show; and every week-end more and more are finding "their feet" and revelling in their new freedom.

A. J. Brown, *Moorland Tramping in West Yorkshire*, 1931

There Must Be Dales in Paradise

... There *must* be dales in Paradise
  Which you and I will find,
  And smile (since God is kind)
At all the foreign peoples there
Enchanted by our blessed air!

There must be dales in Paradise
  With noble tops atween:
  Swart fells uprearing to the skies
  And stretching to the green
And ower t'tops we two shall go,
Knee-deep in ling or broom or snow!

There must be inns in Paradise
  Where nappy ale is sold,
  And beef and pickels – even Pies
  Such as we've known of old!
And we will find a parlour there
  And call for pints for all to share!

A. J. Brown, from *Four Boon Fellows*, 1928

The Escape to the Dales

However poor you are in Bradford, you need never be walled in, bricked up, as around a million folk must be in London. Those great bare heights, with a purity of sky above and behind them, are always there, waiting for you. And not very far beyond them, the authentic dale country begins. There is no better country in England. There is everything a man can possibly want in these dales, from trout streams to high wild moorland walks, from deep woods to upland miles of heather and ling. I know of no other countryside that offers you such entrancing variety.

So if you can use your legs and have a day now and then to yourself, you need never be unhappy long in Bradford. The hills and moors are there for you. Nor do they wait in vain. The Bradford folk have always gone streaming out to the moors. In the old days, when I was a boy there, this enthusiasm for the neighbouring country had bred a race of mighty pedestrians. Everybody went on enormous walks. I have known men who thought nothing of tramping between thirty and forty miles every Sunday. In those days the farmhouses would give you a sevenpenny tea, and there was always more on the table than you could eat. Everybody was knowledgeable about the Dales and their walks, and would spend hours discussing the minutest details of them. You caught the fever when you were quite young, and it never left you. However small and dark your office or warehouse was, somewhere inside

Escape to the Dales. A large group on a day's outing pauses for tea at the entrance to Gordale Scar *(**Alan Stockdale collection**)*

156

your head the high moors were glowing, the curlews were crying, and there blew a wind as soft as if it came straight from the middle of the Atlantic. This is why we did not care very much if our city had no charm, for it was simply a place to go and work in, until it was time to set out for Wharfedale or Wensleydale again. We were all, at heart, Wordsworthians to a man. We have to make an effort to appreciate a poet like Shelley, with his rather gassy enthusiasm and his bright Italian colouring; but we have Wordsworth in our very legs.

J. B. Priestley, *English Journey*, 1933

Darrowby

It was hot in the rickety little bus and I was on the wrong side where the July sun beat on the windows. I shifted uncomfortably inside my best suit and eased a finger inside the constricting white collar. It was a foolish outfit for this weather....

The driver crashed his gears again as he went into another steep bend. We had been climbing steadily now for the last fifteen miles or so, moving closer to the distant blue swell of the Pennines. I had never been in Yorkshire before but the name had always raised a picture of a county as stodgy and unromantic as its pudding: I was prepared for solid worth, dullness and a total lack of charm. But as the bus groaned its way higher I began to wonder. The formless heights were resolving into high grassy hills and wide valleys. In the valley bottoms, rivers twisted among the trees and solid grey-stone farmhouses lay among islands of cultivated land which pushes bright green promontories up the hillsides into the dark tide of heather which lapped from the summits.

I had seen the fences and hedges give way to dry stone walls which bordered the roads, enclosed the fields and climbed endlessly over the surrounding fells. The walls were everywhere, countless miles of them, tracing their patterns high on the green upland....

I realised the bus was clattering along a narrow street which opened on to a square where we stopped. Above the window of an unpretentious grocer shop I read "Darrowby Co-operative Society". We had arrived.

I got out and stood beside my battered suitcase, looking about me. There was something unusual and I couldn't put my finger on it at first. Then I realised what it was – the silence. The other passengers had dispersed, the driver had switched off his engine and there was not a sound or movement anywhere. The only visible sign of life in the centre of the square was a group of old men sitting round the clock tower in the centre of the square but they might have been carved from stone.

Darrowby didn't get much space in the guide books but when it was mentioned it was described as a grey little town on the river Darrow with a cobbled market place and little of interest except its two ancient bridges. But when you looked at it, its setting was beautiful on the pebbly river where the houses clustered thickly and straggled unevenly along the lower slopes of Herne Fell. Everywhere in Darrowby, in the streets, through the windows of the houses you could see the Fell rearing its calm, green bulk more than two thousand feet above the huddled roofs.

There was a clarity in the air, a sense of space and airiness that made me feel I had shed something on the plain, twenty miles behind me. The confinement of the city, the grime, the smoke – already they seemed to be falling away from me.

James Herriot. *If Only They Could Talk*, 1970

Malham before the tourist invasion. It would be hard today to find such a peaceful moment, with just a small flock of sheep being driven through the centre of the village

Sunday Afternoon in Malhamdale

Nowadays visitors have replaced sheep as a source of Malharn's prosperity. They come to this dale from many parts of the West Riding at weekends and on public holidays. The green at Malham on a hot Sunday afternoon in summer resembles a seaside beach, with fancy-dressed visitors, picnic parties, impromptu dances to the ever-present transistor, family games of cricket, sun-bathers, some earnest elderly walkers who disdain hiking regalia and many pseudo-potholers who carry enough equipment to descend a hundred potholes but who rarely move from the green. As a background to all this, instead of the fisherman's nets of seaside resorts there is a fringe of bicycles, scooters, up-to-the-minute motor cycles and ancient cars, for modern youth must be mobile and these weekend visitations are, save for the few elderly earnest walkers, mainly youthful – and noisy. By evening the crowds begin to move away, for they have to return to Leeds, Bradford, Keighley, York. The noise dies down and apart from the late roar of a group of motor cycles or a late-dawdling car changing gear on one of the hilly roads home, somewhere around midnight peace descends upon the dale, the caterers "side away" the last plates and dishes, local residents come to their doors for a reassurance that peace has returned to the dale and probably shake their heads over the day's litter deposits. Somewhere an owl hoots in the stillness. In a moment the ancient dale slips back a thousand years almost unchanged.

Harry J. Scott, *Portrait of Yorkshire*, 1965

Beautiful Beyond Words

I suppose everyone has a piece of landscape somewhere that he finds captivating beyond words and mine is the Yorkshire Dales. I can't altogether account for it because you can easily find more dramatic landscapes elsewhere, even in Britain. All I can say is that the Dales seized me like a helpless infatuation when I first saw them and will not let me go.

Partly I suppose, it is the exhilarating contrast between the high fells, with their endless views, and the relative lushness of the valley floors, with their clustered villages and green farms, To drive almost anywhere in the Dales is to make a constant transition between the hypnotic zones. It is wonderful beyond words. And it partly is the smug air of self-containment that the enclosing hills give, a sense that the rest of the world is far away and unnecessary, which is something you come to appreciate very much when you live there.

Bill Bryson, *Notes from a Small Island* 1995

Pedal power vintage style! A cycling expedition - complete with tandem - pauses on Burnsall village green
(Alan Stockdale collection)

Nature in her Glory

The Making of the Landscape

Looking specially to the action of water now running in the valleys, we observe that the very channel is marked by peculiarities of the same kind, and depending on the same conditions. To instance only the most beautiful of the peculiarities of our northern rivers, the "forces" and rapids which impart so much interest to the Valley of the Yore. In accompanying many little streams which descend from the moors, several hundred feet before they reach the river, we find at almost every point where limestone beds rest upon shale, and often where sandstone beds take the similar position, a step in the channel, over which the water falls a few inches, a few feet, or many yards, according to circumstances. Each of these little cascades is subject to displacement. The limestone beds are slightly worn away and excavated by the sharp sands and pebbles which the stream brings downwards, but this is a feeble element of change. A more powerful effect is occasioned when the rock is *undermined* by the more rapid waste of the shale, and it consequently breaks off at one of the more numerous natural joints, and falls. Thus that operation by which Niagra has been removed, and is undergoing removal, which has furnished to Sir C. Lyell most interesting reflections, may be witnessed on hundreds of streams in Yorkshire. The scale is microscopic, indeed, but its results are of the same order, fully as instructive and not less impressive on the mind.

The mere action of the humid and variable atmospheres of England is wasting, every hour, the surfaces of what are vainly thought to be eternal hills. Even the drop of rain cannot be traced from the cloud, over the surface and through the substance of rocks to its exit in a spring, without teaching us that these rocks are continually undergoing waste, and that this waste is proportional to the nature of the rocks. Rain-drops bring down carbonic acid, and thus exert a chemical as well as mechanical action. In favourable circumstances, the actual channels which they make are preserved. On the wide and bare surfaces around Ingleborough and Penyghent, and on Hutton Roof Crags, west of Kirkby Lonsdale, these channels are innumerable, of all breadths and depths, and of length and direction depending on the slope and continuity of the masses. Where the strata are level, the little ramifications of the rainchannels run deviously, and terminate in the numerous natural joints; but where, as on Hutton Roof Crags, the strata acquire a steep arched slope, the channels take the direction of the slope, run together as valleys do, and collect into miniature dales, till some great fissure lying across their path swallows them up. Below this joint, other channels commence to be in their turn swallowed up.

The fissures here indicated are natural joints of the rock, produced by contraction during its consolidation; they are often symmetrically disposed (prevalent directions are N.N.W. and E.N.E.), and by dividing the mass of limestone present easy passages downward for water. Thus Malharn Tarn delivers itself, not by a surface channel, but by subterranean passages; the river Nid is swallowed up near Lofthouse: streams which gather on the moorland fells, sink into smaller holes of the limestone below, or wind through subterranean caverns. These fissures, by giving passage to water, suffer enlargement so as to become rifts between cliffs, or channels round insulated peaks or jutting crags. Gordale, a good example of these effects, will again attract our attention.

When the fissures have one prevalent direction, the rock is split into vertical plates: a second section of joints develops prisms in these. Large joints, thus crossing at intervals, produce huge vertical masses, which, in consequence of the removal of adjoining parts, often stand out like prominent towers of a Cyclopean fortress. Kilnsey Crag is a well known example in Wharfedale.

John Phillips, *Rivers, Mountains and Sea Coast of Yorkshire*, 1853

Limestone pavement above Conistone, Upper Wharfedale. As John Phillips succinctly observed more than a century ago: 'The mere action of the humid and variable atmospheres of England is wasting the surfaces of what are vainly thought to be eternal hills' *(Geoff Lund)*

Kilnsey Crag, which has been likened to 'a Cyclopean fortress' *(Dan Binns)*

The Discovery of Dent Fault

Near that part of this (Pennine) range where the carboniferous mountains begin to present a decided escarpment towards the west, commences a great longitudinal fault (or perhaps a system of faults) which has been traced by Mr. Phillips from the heart of Craven to the hills of Kirkby Lonsdale and excellently described in a paper published in a former volume of our *Transactions*. I must refer to this paper that the great Craven Fault has rent asunder a part of the Carboniferous chain, and produced such a downcast on the west side, that mountain masses of limestone are tumbled into the neighbouring regions with an inverted dip; and that there a coalfield which ought to appear above the top of Ingleborough has sunk below the level of its base.

From beneath this coal field the limestone beds again rise up, and, after passing in the form of a great ark over Farlton Knot, recover their horizontal position, and are prolonged into the tabular hills mentioned above which form the south western skirt of the Cumbrian mountains. From which it appears, that the southern calcareous zone of the Cumbrian system is cut off from the central chain by the intervention of the Craven fault.

I once imagined that this great fault ranged through the neighbourhood of Kirkby Lonsdale and Farlton Knot and there terminated. It is unquestionable that the lines of dislocation do range in the direction here indicated (as is proved by the position of the limestone of Kirkby Lonsdale bridge, and the still more remarkable position of the limestone between Casterton and Barbon); but after several subsequent visits to the neighbourhood I found that the local branch of the Craven Fault ranged along the line of junction of the central chain which skirts the Cumbrian system, passing along the south flank of Casterton Low Fell up Barbondale, then across the valley of Dent, through the upper part of the valley of Sedbergh, and along the flank of Bowfell and Wildboar Fell, and the ridge between Mallerstang and Ravenstone Dale; and that along the whole of this line there are enormous and most complex dislocations. Some of these I hope to describe more at length in future communication; and for the present I only observe that a great upheaving force acting at once upon two contiguous and unconformable systems, produced a great strain and separation of parts, accompanied with fractures and dislocations, principally along the line of their junction.

In a part of the range between Mallerstang and Ravenstone Dale, the cluster of the older mountains, by deflecting to the north west, quits the central carboniferous chain; and it becomes a question of some consequence to determine the further range and nature of the great Craven fault. The ruptures produced by it are fortunately on a scale too great to be overlooked or misunderstood. It ranges through Mallerstang into the hills immediately south east of Kirkby Stephen, and those skirting the escarpment which travels towards Stainmoor, and finally stops near the foot of the mountain pass. Its progress is marked by a lofty ridge of carboniferous limestone, which has been upheaved from the very base of the whole system, contorted and shattered, and then sent headlong into the valley, where it is seen as an edge for many miles, and where its lower extremities lie buried under accumulations of alluvial matter and the horizontal conglomerates of the new red sandstone.

Adam Sedgwick, "On the General Structure of the Cumbrian Mountains", *Transactions of the Geological Society of London,*
Vol IV (2nd Series), 1838

The Green Mantle of the Dales

Throughout the north-western district, distinctions appear between the vegetable coverings of the slaty, basaltic, calcareous, shaly and gritstone tracts, and sometimes they are obvious and even striking. Wherever the gritstone rocks rise to high ground they are thickly covered by heath, and often wrapped in deep and ancient peat; beneath a craggy summit of such grit, runs a bluish green herbage of sedges, rushes, and grass, on a slope of argillaceous shale; and very often beneath or amidst these contrasted tints are bands of beautiful short green herbage, the gift of limestone rocks. Even to the very summit of Mickle Fell, Cam Fell, and other high points, the limestone retains this superiority in character, and may thus be traced to the brows of Wharnside and Pennigent, across the thick heath which enveloped the gritstone.

The hue and quality of the herbage on the peaty tracts vary; some of the Hougill Fells have the bluish green sedgy herbage; others are heathy.

The district is only partially wooded; it is chiefly in the lower parts of the valleys, where millstone grit is divided by the rivers, at elevations less than 600 feet above the sea, the mountains and valleys are generally bare of trees.

... *Vicinity of limestone at Settle* – Saxifrages abound

Opposite The green mantle of the Dales, with valley-bottom meadows giving way to pasture and then the sedgy herbage of the fell tops *(Geoff Lund)*
Right Traditional meadow near Burtersett photographed in 1971. It has now gone, along with the pignut, wood cranesbill and many other flowers that were part of it. Agricultural intensification in the 1960s and '70s led to the demise of many such meadows, although ironically those that remain are now fiercely protected *(Marie Hartley)*

in this limestone district, and a second locality of *Dryas Octupetala* is in Arncliffe Dale. The *Lady's Slipper* is also among the rarities of this magnificent mountain district.

Bolton Abbey – In the shales and gritstones of this part of the valley of the Wharfe, occur *Limosella Aquatica* and *Teverium Scordium*.

Henry Baines, *The Flora of Yorkshire*, 1840

The Bird's Eye Primrose

REGINALD FARRER *was born in 1880 at Ingleborough Hall, Clapham, where his interest in gardening on his father's estate created a passion for rare and unusual plants, which led to his becoming one of the world's great plant collectors and botanists. After leaving Oxford, he travelled extensively in Europe, China, Japan, Ceylon and the Himalayas, bringing many rare and exotic species back to Europe for the first time. Many of the great botanic collections, such as the Royal Botanic Gardens in Edinburgh, benefited from Farrer's collections, and at least one popular garden alpine – Farrer's Gentian – recalls its discoverer. As well as being an avid explorer, he was a capable painter, novelist and topographer, and his book* My Rock Garden *is now a much sought-after classic. He died at the tragically early age of 40 during an expedition in the mountains of Burma, catching diphtheria during an extended period of bad summer weather.*

Primula farinosa is the "Meibuts" of North Western England, and the centre of its distribution is the mountain-masses of Ingleborough. From the days of my remotest childhood, when my anxiety was always whether I should return to the country in time to see it, *Primula farinosa* has been my best friend among English wild-flowers. Such a gallant little thing it is, and so fragrant, and so dainty, and altogether so lovable. It is a thriving species, too, increasing by leaps and bounds, until places where ten years ago there wasn't a single plant are now stained

Bird's Eye Primrose (**wood engraving by Marie Hartley)**

purple with it in spring. You cannot frequent this country without seeing it, for not only does it swarm on the mountains in places, but it covers the railway cuttings in the valley below, and here and there makes great patches of colour on the very highway sides, growing so stout and strong that you can scarcely believe that it is not some vigorous show Verbena, with solid heads of blossom. All through winter nothing is seen but a round, fat bud. Then, with spring, unfold the mealy little grey leaves, in themselves a joy. And then June begins, up go the white stems, and out come the semi-globular trusses of lovely pink, golden-eyed flowers, looking so sweet and friendly there is no resisting them. A curious characteristic it has, too, which shows how it still remembers the alpine and glacial period. For in the high places it hurries eagerly into bloom, as early as it can, like a true alpine, anxious to get its flowering over safely in the brief flash of summer, before the glacial winter descends again; while in the valleys and on the rich railway cuttings it makes no such hurry, but takes its own time about blossoming. So that, while the Scars are pink with it, you will not find as much as a bud in the warm lands beneath, until the hill-plants have all withered and gone to seed.

Reginald Farrer, *My Rock Garden*, 1907

The Lily of the Valley

In the green coverts of the crag-crowned wood,
    With tiny bells and pale,
Springs (while the wild-rose yet is in the bud)
    The lily of the vale.

There it unfolds, afar from mountain-meadow,
    Its modest mien and dress;
And makes within the silent, sylvan shadow
    A fairy loveliness.

Not where the tulip shows its glowing splendour,
    Not where the wallflower blooms;
Nor where the rose, with petals bright and tender,
    Exhales its sweet perfumes

Not to the public eye – but under cover
    Of rock and branches near,
it gives its gentle charms to Nature's lover,
    In its appointed sphere.

Not with the sky's deep hue is its adorning,
    Nor rainbow-colours bright;
Not with the crimson flush of rising morning,
    But with its own pure white.

Though oft with modest grace its bells it raises
    Where seldom foot hath trod;
Yet in obedience to His laws, it praises
    The power and love of God.

And we may learn a lesson from its beauty,
    Shown in its lonely place
That each, in its own lot of life and duty,
    May glorify God's grace.

Henry Lea Twistleton, 1875

The Early Purple Orchid on Ingleborough

The Early Purple Orchid is not uncommon on the lower slopes of Ingleborough towards Ribblehead, and it is a welcome announcer that spring has come; indeed in some years it is in flower at the same time as the wood anemone and Lesser Celandine and the huge snowdrops which can be found in the woods but which persist here very much later than in the south. I've sometimes wondered whether *The Times* would take a letter from me headed 'The Last Snowdrop', affirming that my snowdrops were blooming in June....... Hereabouts too, close beside and in the streams that come off the side of the hill, and on the lower slopes, as early as March but lasting into May, the Marsh Marigolds (or Molly Bobs or King Cups) abound, especially if it has been a very wet February. Much later their less blatant and more sophisticated friend, but no close relation, the Globe Flower appears in the wet grass. In late summer my favourite can be found, Grass of Parnassus, standing erect among reedy grasses, proudly displaying its now perfect flower, a white five-petalled cup with slight green veins.

Harry Rée, *The Three Peaks* 1983.

Flora of the Dales
Left Grass of Parnassus, a favourite
plant standing erect among reedy
grasses, proudly displaying its white
five-petalled flower with
slight green veins

Opposite, top Bird's Eye Primrose,
with its 'trusses of lovely pink,
golden-eyed flowers, looking so
sweet and friendly'.

Opposite, bottom Globe Flower,
photographed at Marsett on the top
side of Semerwater
(Marie Hartley - 3)

169

The Destruction of the Lady's Slipper Orchid

In the Arncliffe valley the history of the Lady's Slipper has been even darker. The Arncliffe valley is a very narrow mountain glen, with steep fells rising through woods on either side towards the great moorlands overhead. It runs due north out of Skipton, and ends, a blind alley, under the eastern slope of Penyghent far above and out of sight. Here, in these mountain copses, ever since the time of Withering, the Cypripedium has been known. And one old vicar kept a careful watch over it, and went every day to pluck the flowers and so keep the plant safe, for without the flower you might if uninstructed, take the plant for a Lily of the Valley. Then one year he fell ill. The plant was allowed to blossom; was discovered uprooted without mercy, and there was an end of him. And worse was to follow: for a professor from the north – I will not unfold whether it were Edinburgh, or Glasgow or Aberdeen, or none of these, that produced this monster of men – put a price on the head of Cypripedium, and offered the inhabitants so much for every rooted plant they sent him. The valley accordingly was swept bare, and, until the patient plant was rediscovered last year, there was nothing left to tell of the glen's ancient glory except one clump of the Cypripedium which, to keep it holy, had been removed to the vicarage garden, there to maintain, in a mournful but secure isolation, the bygone traditions of Arncliffe.... Accursed for evermore, into the lowest of the Eight Hot Hells, be all reckless uprooters of rarities, from professors downwards....

Reginald Farrer, *My Rock Garden*, 1905

Nature Observed in Wild Places

RICHARD KEARTON, (1862-1928), *was born in Thwaite, Swaledale; crippled in childhood through medical neglect, his chance meeting with a London publisher on the moors led to Richard, and later his brother Cherry, achieving world-wide fame as naturalists, photographers, writers and broadcasters.*

I love my mother's country in the heart of Fell-land with a passion that can never die. Its fresh, cool breezes, grey limestone crags, and chattering becks tumbling over mossy boulders, appeal to me with the same instinctive longing that sends a little bird over a thousand miles of sea and land to the beloved old hedgerow in which it first followed its tiny wings and learnt something of the freedom of the air.

Thither let us journey and tarry for a while amongst our feathered friends in their peaceful haunts, far, far away from the hum and turmoil of men.

From one cause or another the wild life of any given district ebbs and flows if it be watched carefully over a series of years. The peewit, or lapwing, used to be one of the commonest birds on the fells a few years ago, but the barbaric fashion of eating the bird and its eggs at the same season has reduced its numbers far below those of the curlew in the same districts. This is very regrettable from the bird-lovers' point of view, but as the lapwing is one of the farmer's most useful allies in the production of human food, there is another and far more serious aspect of the case to be considered.

The upper reaches of the River Eden are rich in bird life. Picture to yourself a few acres of more or less flat ground – an old-time deposit of the river in mighty flood. It is besprinkled with tufts of rushes and encroaching patches of bracken, with here and there a moss-gown boulder peeping out in forlorn isolation. On either hand it is flanked by steeply rising green hills studded all over with outcrops of grey limestone. Through the middle the river meanders, a mere trickle shining in the sunlight like a snail's silvery trail, wearing away when in spate first one bank then the other, making excellent breeding-places for innumerable sand martins that skim and twirl over its pools and rippling shallows all the livelong day, and you will be able to visualise the headquarters of the sandpiper and yellow wagtail in the months of May and June.

Two hundred yards further up-stream the water tumbles through a rocky gorge. Here it is so cabined and confined that it rushes in a white jet down into a rocky funnel fifteen feet deep. In dry weather this giant funnel is never quite full, because the water escapes through a hole in its lower rim and bubbles up in the deep pool below, making it look like the surface of that of a boiling kettle. Of course, in flood time a lot of the stream is spilt over the rim of the funnel, and, meeting the current rushing from below, creates a great turmoil.

Here you can always find a pair of dippers breeding in perfect safety on the upper edge of a damp, unapproachable slope of an overhung rock forming the far side of the funnel, and quite above the high-water mark of anything but an abnormal flood. If you attempted to swim to it across the pool the chances are you would not be able to scramble up its steep, slippery side, and might be sucked to destruction by the volume of water dragging for ever downwards towards hole in the lower rim.

A few yards overhead there is a small inaccessible limestone crevice in the face of the limestone cliff. In this the beautiful grey wagtail, with its canary yellow breast and long, black tail, has bred from time immemorial.

Fifty yards higher up the gorge is spanned by an old wooden footbridge in the very last stages of decreptitude. Its timbers are so deeply decayed that it would hardly be safe for two people to cross at the same time, lest it should collapse and precipitate them headlong into the unlighted depths of the narrow rock-pool beneath.

A little way below the funnel hole the river meanders over a shingle bank and tumbles into another deep pool crowded with trout of all ages and sizes. In droughty weather you can see them through the six or seven feet of limpid water all lying at rest, like a regiment of soldiers, every head pointing upstream. In these congregations the

A lapwing and its chicks. The famous naturalist Richard Kearton noted that 'the barbaric fashion of eating the bird and its eggs at the same season has reduced its numbers far below those of the curlew' **(David Binns)**

small fish are compelled to keep an ever-wary eye on the larger ones, because old trout have a disagreeable habit of turning cannibal. I have seen, nay caught, in the days of my youth, when tickling was not regarded as poaching and trout far more plentiful than in these by-law-bound times, a fish a foot and a half long with another in its mouth so large it could not be swallowed, and had to be digested piecemeal. A hungry, unsophisticated trout will rise at anything he can swallow. On one occasion I tickled a pounder from beneath the dark recesses of an overhanging bank, and discovered he had just sucked down an innocent little water shrew as he swam across a pool no wider than the surface of an ordinary-sized dining table.

Richard Kearton, *At Home with Wild Nature*, 1922

To a Dipper

Thi bonny briest's as white as sna'
    It's pure, ay, lily pure;
An' puts i't'shade them bau's o' foam
    At sails away doon Eure.

Yan wonders whaur thoo's bin te skeul,
    Thoo's gey weel trained, Ah lay,
Fer Curtsey efter curtsey
    Thoo's gi'en te me teday.

Thoo cooers doon this way an' that,
    Thoo's weel-behaved, fer seur;
Yan nivver kna's just what's astir,
    It's grand to be at t'deur.

Er noo thoo sings thi gloamin' song,
    'Mang singers thoo's a swell:
Here, back o't'wau, Ah hev, thoo kn's
    A concert te misel'.

Thaur, keepen time wi' t'tinklen streeam,
    Thoo's nivver nivver flat;
Thoo's full o' tune wi'oot a doot,
    Ah'll allus stick te that.

Ah'd like te shoot "gan on mi lass",
    Thoo weel desarves a clap;
But if Ah did thoo'd pop up t'beck
    Fair scaured at sike a whap.

Thoo's weathered t'stooren, blisteren blast,
    Ah's seur Ah's varra fain;
Good-day fair Peggy, some day seun
    Ah s'mak this way again.

An' when at heeame teneet Ah lig
    Mi heead doon o' me pilla',
An' odd lang thowt, lass, be o' thee,
    A white throat on' a willa'.

John Thwaite, 1873-1941

172

Above Nature in her glory - inspired by Upper Nidderdale
Opposite Dipper
(***paintings by David Binns***)

173

A Place for Ravens

I sought the ravens at dawn, a time of great activity. The birds had fasted for nine hours. Search about among the boulders at the base of crags on which ravens roost and you will find small, compact pellets which the birds have ejected – neat bundles of indigestible remains of the last meals. One pellet I broke open contained beetles, sheep wool, tufts of grass and pieces of coarse grit. The hunger calls of young ravens at dawn are stilled only when ample food has been provided, when a bird's stomach is round and firm as a drum.

Ravens are faithful to a number of nesting sites, at one of which a nest is refurbished for a new season. Almost all the Pennine nests are on crags. The nests are bulky, formed of substantial twigs taken from the nearest trees, thorn or rowan. Heather is added, and the nest is usually upholstered with sheep wool.

I followed a sheep-trod along the edge of the hill. It extended on a comfortable gradient for walking, and sheep movement had kept the way clear of the coarse and draggly vegetation that elsewhere on the hillside would have wrapped itself round my ankles. The sharp cleaves of sheep, scouring the rocks, also kept the route well defined even when I crossed a scree slope. Half an hour later I reached the line of limestone cliffs on which are the soggy remains of old raven nests and, I confidently hoped, the nest of the year.

The cliff range, which had been continuous, was now badly eroded. Promontories of light grey rock were thatched with coarse grass. Between them, gullies scoured deeply by rain and landslip. Littering the gullies were unstable screes of gritstone that had slithered from the heights – and slithered still.

Sunlight, filtered by mist, gave an illusion of warmth where warmth was absent. A cold wind blew steadily from the north-east, as it had done for days, emanating from a high pressure system centred on the North Sea. A friend who visited the raven crags with three companions during a snowbound February excused himself when the crests of snowdrifts reached as high as his waist. The others went on, gingerly climbing, and found the female raven squatting on the nest. It was the only dark patch on a hill that otherwise was sparklingly white. The raven, emboldened by the cruel weather and the necessity to keep the eggs warm, stayed on the nest and even permitted itself to be stroked.

As I began my ascent of the gully, the deep flight notes of a raven descended from a bird that regarded me gravely as it glided by. A raven is large – rather more than two feet from the tip of its black beak to the end of its graduated black tail – and in flight the wingtips curve upwards a little. The ends of the primary feathers are distinct, like dark fingers clutching the air.

The bird's mate appeared. Both the ravens were vocal in their restlessness. They alighted, but not for long. In their effortless flights on stiffened wings, they made subtle alterations to their trim and thus harnessed the power of an air current that sang on its way up the slopes from the dale.

When I stood on the cliff-edge, the ravens glided by. One bird, banking, alighted on a boulder, hopped, then walked a pace or two. Sunlight gave its undertaker-black plumage a silver sheen. I advanced. The raven opened its wings, and the breeze carried the bird aloft, where its legs remained dangling, assisting it to maintain its balance in the turbulence.

The bird almost closed its wings, diving with something of the verve of a 'stooping' peregrine. When the wings were again opened, and the wind harnessed, the raven was swept high. Twice, in quick succession, it flicked on to its back. I have known ravens fly belly-upwards from the sheer joy of being alive, and one bird glided on its back for upwards of a quarter of a mile across a Yorkshire dale.

From my cliff-edge vantage point I beheld a raven as it swept by against a background of broad acres – the fell edge, pastures, meadows; against wall patterns, outbarns, and sparkling streams. These ravens glided, soared, somersaulted, dived with partly-closed wings or banked to reveal handsome profiles and dangling legs. Their ponderous black beaks had silver highlights, mirroring the sun's brilliance. Pointed throat feathers resembled dark ruffs.

W. R. Mitchell, *Wild Pennines*, 1976

Protecting the Swaledale Wolves

Close by runs the road between Richmond and Marske, and aiming for the latter place we take the turn right and cross the elevated land with Feldom Moor to the right, a grouse-range belonging to Mr Hutton, of Marske, and the large-fir-woods belonging to Lord Zetland on our left. In pre-Norman times this high tract of ground, as well as most of the secluded gills around, literally swarmed with wolves, but when the country at a later period became more populous, and the forest laws were in full force, these savage creatures were not so numerous, and special care was taken by the lords of the forest to preserve them. Thus in 1171 the monks of Jervaulx, who owned the farm and lands at Feldom, received a grant from Earl Conan of Richmond, of free pasturage within his domain of New Forest, stipulating however that no hounds or mastiffs were to be kept there, and that the wolves were not to be driven away from the pastures. If we had all the records, what horrid stories should we have of children and others attacked and devoured by these blood thirsty creatures. The laws were very strict at this time; no one even being allowed to keep any large dog without its being properly expedited, that is, to have three claws cut off each fore-foot to prevent the dog from hunting.

Harry Speight, *Romantic Richmondshire* 1897

Red Grouse *(David Binns)*

The Christian Heritage

Easby Abbey

A beautiful walk downstream from Richmond through woods and water meadows leads to the ruins of the Premonstratensian Easby Abbey of St Agatha. Pevsner thought this 'one of the most picturesque ruins in the county richest in monastic ruins'. Near to the abbey gatehouse and within its walls stands the parish church, whose founding may have pre-dated that of the monastery. This is also dedicated to St Agatha, the serving priest, before the dissolution, always being one of the abbey canons. Within the church is a replica of the Easby Cross (the original is in the Victoria and Albert Museum), the finest example of Anglo-Saxon sculpture (c 800) in Yorkshire. The church also contains, among much of historical and aesthetic interest, wall-paintings from the mid-thirteenth century of Old and New Testament scenes. The connection of the Scrope family with the abbey is recalled by their sculptured arms on the porch of the church next to those of the families of Aske and Conyers. These links with the Roman religion are found again in neighbouring Brough Hall, formerly the seat of the Catholic Lawsons. The hall is at present being converted into modern flats but on rising ground before it stand the family chapel and adjoining presbytery in a state of seemingly sad neglect. It was not very far away, at Catterick, that St Paulinus once baptised converted dalesmen in the running waters of the River Swale.

Peter Gunn, *The Yorkshire Dales: Landscape with Figures* 1983

The Glory that is Departed

A more interesting relic than Jervaulx Abbey, though little more than a ground plan remains, it would be difficult to find; originally founded in 1136, and like other monastic establishments suppressed in 1536. Most thoroughly at that time the spoilers did their work, defiling the holy temple, and making "Jerusalem a heap of stones". The church is unroofed, and the conventual buildings, and the walls in most places razed to the ground. As time rolled the earth accumulated, and the weeds grew in rank luxuriance, so that the once beautiful abbey is almost entirely hidden. Instead of the hymns "Jam Lucis orto sidere" or "Ales diei nuncius" welcoming the morn, no sound was heard, save the note of blackbird or thrush. It might have been truthfully said of the choir from which the loud Hosanna had once rolled and the sacrifice of prayer and praise ascended, 'Ichabod, Ichabod! thy glory is departed."

... A charming walk conducts through green fields and pleasant pastures towards Aysgarth, leaving behind the fairy towers of Bolton Castle; and long before it is reached the noise of the waterfall strikes upon the ear, guiding the direction. There are two waterfalls, but the lower one below the bridge is much the finer, where the Yore falls over three ledges of limestone. What a charming spot on a hot afternoon! What a cool shelter is that afforded by the overhanging rocks! Amid these Arcadian scenes an idyll of Theocritus is pursued, one in which the old bard gives a graphic description of the summer melting into autumn, when the fruit is falling on the ground, and the air resonant with the hum of insect life, making what Virgil, the imitator of Theocritus, calls a "sussuras".

Rev. John Pickford, *A Week in the Yorkshire Dales*, 1869

Jervaulx Abbey in lower Wensleydale. Despite being turned into 'a heap of stones' on the dissolution of the monasteries, there is still much of interest to see *(Marie Hartley)*

The Founders of Fountains Abbey

The awful remains of this ancient Abbey fill the midway of a deep Vale, through which flows the Brook called Skell, and the high Hills on either side clothed with lofty Trees, and varied with Scars, slope gently to the brook.

"In these deep solitude and awful cells,
when heavenly pensive contemplation dwells"

In 1132 certain Benedictine Monks at Saint Mary's in York, displeased with relaxation of discipline in their Convent, and disgusted with the luxury of their life, resolved to migrate where monastic manners were practised with more severity. Much had been said of the austerities of the Monks of the Cistercian Order at Rievaulx, and they determined to embrace the rules of this society, and applied for the purpose to Thurstan, Archbishop of York, whom they requested to favour their designs as well as visit their Abbey, and endeavour to

The west door of the nave at Fountains Abbey - Britain's finest Cistercian monastery

restore discpline to its orginal purity. The Prelate, with many of the Clergy, went to St Mary's where they found the Abbot and his attendants preparing to oppose his resolutions, and threatened to punish the discontented Monks. He was refused admittance into the Chapter House, when a riot ensued, and the Prelate, having interdicted the Abbot and Monks, left the Monastery taking under his protect the Prior, Sub-prior, and eleven Monks, who withdrew from the Convent, and were entertained by the Archbishop for eleven weeks. During this time, the Abbot made frequent complaints to the King, Bishops and Abbots, against the Archbishop for depriving him of part of his flock. Two of them soon afterwards returned, but one of them early repented, and rejoined his companions. The other, fond of Benedictine luxury, continued in the Convent.

At Christmas, Thurstan gave them a place, then called Skelldale, for their residence, the receptable of wild beasts and overgrown with wood and brambles; he also gave them the village of Sutton. Their first Abbot was Richard, their late Prior at St Mary's, who, with the Monks, retired to their desert, resting entirely on Providence for their support. During part of the winter, a large Elm Tree was their only shelter; they afterwards retired under the melancholy shade of seven Yew trees , growing where the Abbey now stands. One of them was blown down in 1757, the other six (1818) standing. They are of great magnificence, the largest being 20 feet in circumference, within three feet from the ground. Under these, it should seem, they resided until the Monastery was built. The fame of their sanctity induced many to resort to them, which proportionally increased their distress, and rendered their poverty still more severe; for in vain did the Abbot solicit relief as famine that year had extended all over the country, and the leaves of trees and herbs, except a small supply from the Archbishop, were their only food. In the midst of all their wants and sufferings, when their provision amounted to only two loaves and a half, a stranger solicited their charity, when the Abbot directed that one of the loaves should be given him, observing that *the Almighty would provide for them*. Soon after, Eustace Fitz-John, Lord of Knaresbrough, supplied them with a cart load of bread. For more than two years they laboured under every hardship poverty could inflict, till Hugh, Dean of York, who was very rich, labouring under a disease likely to prove fatal, resolved to end his days among them. For this purpose he removed to the Abbey, and devoted his riches to Charity, the building of the Monastery and uses of the houses. The world was now all before them.

The Tourist's Companion – a Concise Description and History of Ripon, Studley Park and Fountains Abbey (anon). Ripon, 1818

Hubberholme, one of the most appealing of all Dales churches, photographed in the summer of 1939. Inside, it retains its rood loft and is noted for furnishings by Robert Thompson, the 'mouseman of Kilburn' *(Richard C. Joy)*

The Sermon on Firbank Fell

The Yorkshire Dales occupy a special position in the history of Quakerism, because it was in the Northern Dales that this great world-wide Christian movement began. GEORGE FOX, (1624-90) was the founder of the Friends; his account of the events leading up to his historic sermon on Firbank Fell, near Sedbergh, has the compulsion of momentous events told in vigorous prose.

As so I passed away being among the fell Countreys, and lay out all night, and a stranger and so that the next day I passed upp to a Market town, upon a Market day, and spoke to the people and bid them repent (and take heed of the deceitfull merchandize) and woshippe God in the spirit and truth and so I passed away up winadayle, and declared the truth though all the towns as I went, and people took mee for a madd man and distracted and some followed

179

and questioned with mee and was astonished and then followed me a Schoolemaster and get mee into a house and thought I had been a young man that was gone distracted that was gone away from my parents or thought to have kept mee, but they being astonished at my answers and the truth I spake to them they could not tell what to say, and would have me to have staied all night, but I was not to stay butt passed away (and wandered in the night).

And at last I came to an alehouse where there was some fellows drinking and I walked up and down in the lane and after a time they beganne to drink to mee and then I spake to them the truth and warning them of the mighty day of the lord was comeing and bid them take heed to that which shewed them sin and evill in their hearts upon which one rose against mee with a clubb, and so they held one another, and then they were quiet, I walking out as to have gone to have then all night outdoors; and hee that would have strucke mee followed mee and so I was moved to come into ye house again and so staid with them all night, and the next morning I was moved to tell the man of the house that I was the sonne of God and was come to declare truth to them, and so hee had me down among some professors who after I had declared truth to them and they received it, and they directed mee to other professors.

The inspirational simplicity of the early Quaker meeting house at Brigflatts, near Sedbergh (*Marie Hartley*)

And then I came to one Bousfields (in Gasdaile) who received where there were many convinced, and from thence I was directed to Gervase Benson where there was a meeting of professing people; and I lay at Richard Robinson and speaking to him he was convinced, and the next day being the first day of the week I went down to the meeting, where they were generally carried out that day, and generally received Truth, and came to the teacher with the Christ Jesus.

Presently after there was a great fair to be at Sedbury, near Gervase Benson, where many young people came to be hyred and I went through the fair and spake, and then went to the steeple house yard (and got upp by a tree) and spake to the people largely, many Professors and priests being there; and to bring them off, of their worshipps, to worship God, in the spirit, and had no opposition, but only one Captain which said that the steeple house was the Church, which I told him it was a place of limestone and wood (for the Church was God as in This. 1 and 1) and so after had some few words hee passed away, and the truth came over all, and I was satisfied concerning it; and when I was passing away, one priest said to the people I was distracted, his mouth being stopped by the powers of God for opposeing, that was his only Cover to the People, and so I passed away and had some other meetings upp and down in that Country, when divers were Convinced and received the Truth.

And then I came to ffirbank Chappel, where there was a great meetting of the sober people, of the Country and severall speakers, whence moderate people desired mee not to speak unto the speakers because they are something contrary to the world, and there were many sorts of people there, and so not to speak to them in the steeplehouse; and indeed there was nothing upon me to speak to them; and so afterward when the meeting was done in the forenoon, I went up upon the hill in the afternoone; and the people came to me for the steeple house would not hold them in the morning and some would me want to go into the steeple house as being a strange thing for a man to speak out of the steeplehouse; and so after a while I beganne to speak to the People and all quiet, and the greatest part of a thousand people were convinced that day.

George Fox, *Journal*, 1652

Nonconformity in the Dales. Harvest Festival at Askrigg Moor Road Primitive Methodist Chapel, built in 1869. It closed in 1971 and is now two houses *(Marie Hartley)*

Preaching in Lovely Wensleydale

We crossed over the enormous mountain into lovely Wensleydale, the largest by far of all the Dales as well as the most beautiful. Some years since, many had been awakened here, and joined together by Mr. Ingham and his preachers. But since the bitter discussion between their preachers, the poor sheep have all been scattered. A considerable number of them have been gleaned up and joined together by our preachers. I came into the midst of them at Redmire. As I rode through the town the people stood staring on every side, as if we had been a couple of monsters. I preached in the street, and they soon ran together, young and old, from every quarter. I reminded the elder of their having seen me thirty years before, when I preached in Wensley church; and enforced are we to

"Believe in the Lord Jesus Christ, and thou shalt be saved." When I rode back through the town, it wore a new face. The people were profoundly civil; they were bowing and curtseying on every side. Such a change in two hours I have seldom seen.

Hence we hasted to Richmond, when I preached in a kind of square. All the Yorkshire Militia were there; and so were their officers, who kept them in awe, so that they behaved with decency. At six I preached at the end of our house in Barnard Castle. I was frail and feverish when I began; but the staying an hour in a cold bath (for the wind was very high and sharp) quite refreshed me, so that all my faintness was gone, and I was perfectly well when I concluded.

John Wesley, *Journal*, Tuesday 14th June, 1774

Chapel le Dale Churchyard

The little church, called Chapel-le-Dale, stands about a bow-shot from the family house. There they had all been carried to the font; there they had each led his bride to the altar; and there they had, each in his turn, been borne upon the shoulders of their friends and neighbours. Earth to earth they had been consigned for so many generations, that half of the soil of the church-yard consisted of their remains. A hermit who might wish his grave to be as quiet as his cell, could imagine no fitter resting place. On three sides was an irregular low stone wall, rather to mark the limits of the sacred ground, than to enclose it; on the fourth it was bounded by the brook whose waters proceed by a subterranean channel, from Weathercote Cave. Two or three alders and rowan trees hung over the brook, and shed their leaves and seeds into the stream. Some bushy hazels grew at intervals along the lines of the wall; and a few ash trees as the winds had sown them. To the east and west some fields adjoin it in that state of half-cultivation which gives a human character to solitude: to the south, on the other side of the brook, the common, with its limestone rocks appearing everywhere above ground, extended to the foot of Ingleborough. A craggy hill, feathered with birch, sheltered it from the north.

The turf was as soft and fine as that of the adjoining hills; it was seldom broken so scanty was the population to which it was appropriated; scarcely a thistle or a nettle deformed it, and the few tombstones which had been placed there, were now themselves half-buried. The sheep came over the wall when they listed, and sometimes took shelter in the porch from the storm. Their voices and the cry of the kite wheeling above were the only sounds that were heard there, except when the single bell which hung in its niche over the entrance tinkled for service on the Sabbath day, or with a slower tongue gave notice that one of the children of the soil was returning to the earth from which he sprung.

Robert Southey, *The Doctor*, 1847

Part 3

Looking Forward

Arncliffe Primary Schoool, Littondale, photographed in 1989 when there were twenty-two pupils (*Marie Hartley*)

Paintings and Poems
by
Young Dalesfolk

This 'View' of the past Millennium concludes by looking forward to the next one. As part of the overall project, the Yorkshire Dales Millennium Trust invited Dales schools to participate in an art and poetry competition. The theme reflected the title of the first part of this book 'A Sense of Place', with no less than 174 entries being received from 31 schools. The winning paintings and poems are reproduced on the following pages. Both youngsters and judges found the competition memorable. When one judge asked Jack Lund why he had chosen to paint 'Bales' (page 188), back came a true Dales reply: 'Because they were there.' There was nothing more to be said!

Mark Pounder, age 11, Leyburn Primary School

Bus Journey

The red post bus drove down the dale.

A farmer looked through the window,
And saw that his flock were well.

A boy looked through the window,
And saw Brymor ice-cream shop and felt
hungry.

A writer looked through the window,
And saw a hill with words on it.

A mum looked through the window,
And saw Leyburn market with vegetables,
fruit, cheese and kippers for Dad.

An artist looked though the window,
And saw a beautiful view to paint.

A dog looked through the window,
And saw lots of fields to play in.

A postman looked through the window,
And saw a long path to a house.

A hiker looked through the window,
And saw a big hill with rocks to climb.

A tourist looked through the window,
And saw Bolton Castle, open for visitors.
                        Sophie Johnston

The Old Bridge

The bridge has stood two hundred years
With moss protruding from every crack and stone.
Beneath, the stream dawdles over pebbles peacefully,
The spring's sunshine reflecting on the ripples.
Over-hanging trees coming into bud
Cast shadows over the water's edge :
Pussy willow, catkin bursting into bloom;
Sycamore, ash and chestnut line the banks.

Horse and cart, cattle, motor car -
The bridge has seen them all.
But, built only for the trudging boots of miners,
The only life to cross its lonely path today
Is the occasional sheep and armies of advancing grass,
For it cannot hold the weight of even one man now.

The Dales, a sense of place.

Middle of nowhere,
Three houses clinging together for comfort.
Rain!
Wind!
A smell of dip, muck and air all mixed in one.
The hard cold feeling of limestone,
The cold.

Jack Lund, age 9, Arncliffe Primary School

The Dales
Noisy green
Slimy grey
Squidgy mud
Exciting rain
Fantastic sun
Super quiet
Lovely people.

Above Ben Quirk, age 8, Leyburn Primary School
Right Charlotte Huck, age 5, Kettlewell Primary School
6 May 1999

SUBSCRIBERS

Frederick Ackroyd, Leeds
Mrs V Adams
Mrs Kathleen Agar
Sarah Ainger
Joan & Chris Alder, Threshfield
Barbara Alderson, Darlington
B & J Allen, Todmorden
Jean Mary Allsop, Sheffield
Jean P Anderson, Chesterfield
John & Kay Anderson, Long Melford
Raymond Anderson
Shirley & Don Anderson, Derby
R Andrew, Yedingham
Kiki Angelrath, Strumpshaw
Anna & Neil, Brentwood
Ann Archer, Driffield
Mrs Jean Archer, Harden
Lucy Ardron, Sheffield
Arthur Armistead, Bradford
Norman Armistead, Edinburgh
John & Pam Armitage, Wakefield
Arncliffe CE (VC) Primary School
John R Arnold, Sutton-in-Ashfield
D S Ashbridge, Cogenhoe
Roger Ashby, Guiseley
Barbara Ashmore, Doncaster
Stephen David Ashton, Denby Dale
Malcolm & Hazel Ashworth, Embsay
Stuart Aston, Croydon
Miss June Atkinson, Harrogate
Mary Attwood, Hemel Hempstead

Jean Bagshaw, Leeds
John Bailey, Southampton
Peter Bailey
Mrs M Baines
Tony & Linda Baker, Newcastle
M E P Balme, Mirfield
Berinda D Banks, Mill Hill
Betty Barber, Sheffield
D G Barker, Edinburgh
Robert & Anne Barker & Family,
  West Riding
J Malcolm Barr
Elsie M Barraclough, Louth
Barbara B Barrett CM, St John's,
  Newfoundland
Mrs D L Bartlett, Pangbourne
Mrs Davina R Beard, Shoeburyness
Heather M Beaumont, Hebden
V Beaumont, Bedale
Geoff Beavis, York
Malcolm & Joan Beer, Harrogate
C & J Bell
D C & Mrs J Bell
John S Bell
H L Bennett (In Memory)
Mary & Tom Bennett, Dunedin, NZ
Mr & Mrs T E Bennett, Stevenage
Mrs Muriel Berman, Prestwich
Audrey Berry, Eldwick
Heather Berry, Horbury
John Berry, Colne
Martyn Berry, Sevenoaks
Peter Berry, North Stainley
Eileen D Best, Riseley
E V Bewley, Bishop Auckland
Joyce M Billington, Clifton, Beds
Cdr Bird, Nyewood
E J Birtles, March
Malcolm Black, Alveston
Terry Blacklock, Sprotbrough
Mrs Elsie Blackwell, Gargrave

Mrs P B Blagden, Keighley
David Blair
John R Blakeborough, Leeds
Barbara Blakeway, Sambrook
Simon Blakey
Mrs F Blanchard, Kilndown
Florence G Bland, Gunnerside
Brian Blowers, Kettlewell
Sandra Bohme, Hitchin
John William Bollans, London
Thomas Bruce Bolton, South Nutfield
Elizabeth Boorman, Barkingside
Barbara M S Booth, Leeds
Margaret Borner, Faversham
Eric & Doris Bosley,
  Burley-in-Wharfedale
Mr & Mrs H Bottomley (dec),
  late of Kettlewell
Parl V Bowden, Addingham
K Bowran, Birmingham
Christopher & Audrey Bradford, Elston
Jeremy Bradford & Jane King, Otley
Michael & Eveleigh Bradford, Leeds
John & Margaret Bradley,
  Sutton Coldfield
W Braham, Hemel Hempstead
B Braithwaite-Exley, Austwick
Peter Bratby, Purley, Surrey
Mrs T M Brears, Wakefield
Mrs J M Briggs, Skipton
Pamela R Brink, Westville, South Africa
Dominic Brisby, Bristol
Colin & Anne Broadbent, Batley
Denis Brockbank, Wakefield
Rodney Brooke CBE DL, Ilkley
Mrs J F Broughton
A & J Brown, Leeds
M A Brown, Bury St Edmunds
S J Brown, Ramsey
Soren Buhl, Middelfart, Denmark
Rene Bulmer, Yeadon
Joan Burgess, Pannal, Harrogate
Gillian Burland
B Burton, Ilkley
Dawn & Jim Burton, Ilkley
Mrs M Busfield, Corby
Margaret Bush, Driffield
Betty Bushell
Mrs A Butterfield, Mytholmroyd
Betty Buttrick, Eastrington

D & G Cairns
Mrs Elizabeth Caley, Oundle
L Jane Calverley, Connecticut
S R & K Calverley
Barry Carmichael, Hull
Mr & Mrs Carr, Walton-on-Thames
Sheila Carr, Watford
D N Carrick
Norma & Anthony Carruthers,
  Chaddesden
D A Cash, Oxford
W Q & I Casson, Guisborough
Pauline M Castle, Pool-in-Wharfedale
M B Cawood
T A Chalmers
Alice Chamley, Stockport
Gillian M Chapman, Salesbury
Julia Chapman
K Chapman, Burley in Wharfedale
Mrs E M F Charlston, Swillington
D Barbara Charlton, Blackpool
Harry William Charnock, Cheadle

Richard Cheetham
Nicholas Cheetham
Carol & Philip Chubb, Didcot
Clapham C of E Primary School
G A W Clark, West Witton
Roger Clarke, Sheringham
C L Clarkson, Linton
N J Clarkson, Sheffield
Mrs J W Clifford
Jack Clift, Crowle
Cynthia Clifton, Hemingford Grey
Rod Clough, Oldham
Doug & Lyn Coates, Harrogate
Miss J A Cocker, Chudleigh, Devon
Miss D M Coldbeck
John Collins, Beckenham
Sheila & Terry Commins, Middleham
Con and Chris - To our dearest sister
Mrs D Cook
C C Cooke
Mrs H E Cooke
Richard & Elizabeth Cordingley,
  Cawthorne
Jean C Corlett, Ramsey, Isle of Man
Mrs Maureen Costin, Doncaster
  (In Memory)
P Coughtrey, Kings Langley
Walter E Coulson, Welburn, York
M A Cowlard, Stratford-upon-Avon
R S & K Cowley, Rochdale
Jane M Cox, Leeds
Janet Cox, Huntingdon
W G J Cox, Stillington
Joan Crabtree, Kettlewell
Kate Crennell, Chilton, Oxon
G B & J Crompton, Yeadon
Ann & Roy Cross, Doncaster
Damian Crosse, Ilkley
Margaret Crossley, Shipley
Rebecca & Paul Crowell, Salem,
  MA, USA
John Cumberland
Jeannette Curry, Brighton
John & Betty Cusden, Northampton
Sylvia Cuss, Birkenshaw
Barbara & Peter Cussons, Ilkley

John Dalby
Charles & Lois Darnley, Wakefield
M P Dauncey, Ruthin
Elsie Davis (in memory)
S J Davis
Valerie Davis (nee Heptonstall),
  Vancouver, BC
Helga Deak, Skipton
Pauline Delius, London
Mrs Joyce Denton, Leeds
Leslie George Derx, Doncaster
E P Dewar, Addingham
Mrs C Dickinson
Mrs Alma Dixon, Kenilworth
Barbara Donaldson
Heather & Mark Donougher, Lilley
Jeremy Double, Bingley
Lawrence & Pat Downey, Bishopdale
Peter Dowthwaite
Elsie Drake, Walton-on-Thames
Mrs N P Drinkwater, York
Cath Drummond, Hebden Bridge
Dr Ian Drummond, Manchester
Mrs M Duck
Mrs B L Duval, Chearsley, Bucks
Vera Dyer, Majacar Playa, Spain

Derick Dyke, Long Stratton
Terry & Sheila Dyson, Bradford

Paula Edgar, Milton Keynes
Mr & Mrs G B Edmondson, Haverigg
Barry Emmett, Greasby, Wirral

Dorothy Fairburn
Janet & Peter Fairs, Horsham
John Anson Farrer
Michael Farrer, Bradford
Peter & Victoria Fattorini, Linton
Peter Faulkner
Amanda Fawcett, Dewsbury
John & Pam Fawcett, Tunstall
Cyril & Winnie Fell, Richmond
Ms P E Field
David Finegan
John & Sue Finn, Limassol, Cyprus
Mrs N Firth
John Fitch, Cambridge
J Fitton, Bedale
Barbara & John Fleming
Ian Fobbester, Preston-under-Scar
Bernard & Ann Foster, Barden
Richard Foster, Kilnsey (R.W.)
Sophie Foster, Marlow, Bucks
Mrs Ann Fox
Dr David B Fox
John & Gwyneth Fox, West Ayton
Linda Foxcroft, Pocklington
Margaret France, Belmont, Australia
Mrs C M Franklin, Stratford-on-Avon
A Fraser, Ilkley
G A Freeman
L Frost, Wetherby
Peter Frost, East Goscote
Mrs J A Fuller
Lady Jacqueline Fulton, Thornton Dale

R Galley
John & Viv Games, Grimsby
Russell Garbutt, Swanland
Gillian & Antonio Garcia, Tunstall
James & Claire Garner, Liverpool
Margaret Garner, Harrogate
Paul & Elizabeth Garner, Harrogate
Jane & John Garrett, Rawdon
Ernest S Gates, Northam
John & Sheila Geale
Ian Trevor Geldard
Prof & Mrs C E Gibson
Roy Gibson, Dewsbury
Major David J Gill, London
Robin N Gill, New Malden
Moira & Ian Gittins, Leeds
Philip Gledhill, Coven
Mr & Mrs David Glover, Loughboro'
Pat Glover of Middleton
Peter Glover of Farnworth
R D Glover, Ossett
Theresa Glynn
Alison & John Goad
Mary & Ian Goldthorpe
Elizabeth Gomm
Chris Gooch, Hugglescote
Mrs V A Goodson
Jane Goodwin
W E & E Gorse
Dr M S Gosden
Richard & Jenny Goswell
J W Gray, Hull
Mrs K Gray, Hurworth

Muriel Gray, Winchester
C R Green, Harpenden
David Green, Woodnewton
Mrs Lily Greenwood, Wakefield
Stan & Gitti Greenwood, Wakefield
Barry R Gregory, Newby, Scarboro'
Arthur Grimshaw, Bradford
S K Grimshaw
H J Groves, Coylton

John & Julia Hadrill, Vancouver
Gordon Haigh, Wakefield
Peggy Haley, Austwick
Janet E Hall, Brighouse
June Hall, Pilmoor
Mrs M Hall, Hartshead Moor
Susan Hallam, Wigston
S Halls, Hornsea
Linda Halpern
Mr & Mrs R E Halstead, Harrogate
Dr Janet Hamilton, Nanaimo, BC
Ionne, Justin & Erica Hammond,
  Suffolk
R G Hammond, Southbourne
Mark & Heather Hancock, Arncliffe
D M P & C Hanson, Baildon
Miss J M Hanson
Richard Hanwell, Harrogate
Duncon Hare, Dishforth
Douglas Hargreaves, Leeds
Nora Harkin, Batley
Jill Harris, Portsmouth
P D Harrison, Audlem
Thelma Harrison, Harrogate
Marquess of Hartington
Betty & Douglas Hartley, Bradford
C S Hartley, Menston
R S Hartley, Hindhead, Surrey
G & M Hatfield, Doncaster
Tim Hawkes, Lancaster
Right Rev David Hawkin, Bishop of
  Repton, & Mrs E A Hawkin
A R & L N Hayward, Skeeby
Mrs B Head
Mr & Mrs C Heane, Prudhoe
John Heap, Southgate, London
W Allan Heap
Joyce Hellawell, Mytholmroyd
David G Helm
Mr & Mrs John Henry, Bradley
Mr & Mrs C F Hepworth
Mr & Mrs P N Hepworth, York
Robert Heseltine
Mrs Eunice Hewitson, Cheadle
George Hill, Horsforth
Jean Hill, Huddersfield
Dr R A Hill
Richard & Elizabeth Hill,
  Chipping Barnet
J & B Hills
Malcolm Hilton, Mirfield
Patricia Hinds, South Elmsall
M Hird, Huddersfield
Mrs Margaret Hirst, Worcester
Winifred Hodge
Ann Hodgson, London
C Hodgson, Kingston, Ontario
Martyn & Violet Hodgson, Evesham
Ian G Hogbin MBE, Crofton
Jack Hogg, Guiseley
James Kay Holcomb, Urbana, Ohio
Lawrence Holden
Mrs Susan Holland
Bryan Holliday
Mrs M V Hollingworth
B Holmes, Dewsbury
David G Holmes, Wyke

Philip & Deborah Holmes, Leeds
Elaine & Tim Holt, Purley
William Edmund Holt
Stephen Holtby, Beverley
J Hone
Michael Horsfall
R W Hough, Long Eaton
Dan & Anne House
Carol & Michael Howard, Great Asby
Mary S Howcroft, Leeds
Peter & Linda Howells, Harrogate
Mary Hudson, Waltham, Grimsby
Pat Hudson, Ilkley
Joyce Hudspith
Rowena Hughes, Barry
Jane R Hunt
David & Christine Hunter
Ian R Hunter, London
Sheila Hurst, Sandhurst
Colin Hutchinson, Leeds
Suzanne Evelyn Hutley,
  St Leonards-on-Sea

Mrs J Ibbotson
Harold Illingworth (in memory)
Dennis Ingham
Gloria Inman, Blackpool
F A Inness, born Croft Spa
Esme Isherwood, Barden (in memory)

Mr & Mrs D T A Jack, Bolton
Ashley Jackson
Audrey Jackson, Burley-in-Wharfedale
Audrey Mary Jackson
Sarah Jackson
James, Braintree
Lady James of Rusholme
Brian Jenkinson, Doncaster
A S Jennings
Joan & Pearl, York
Mr & Mrs E Johns, Menston
Mr & Mrs R Johns, Hackney
Bryan Johnson, Appleton Roebuck
James E Johnson, Knaresborough
Jean Johnson
K Johnson
Philip & Roda Johnson, Grassington
Mrs W Johnston (Barbara & Valerie)
David & Dorothy Jones, Radcliffe
Jean Jones, Scotton
Maureen Jones, Rayleigh
Sheila M Jones, Doncaster
Jean Joynes, Knaresborough
C Joynt, Sutton on Sea

Mrs F E Kay, Sandal, Wakefield
Mrs G Kay
N B Kaye
Ronald Kear, Crestview, Florida
Lana Ruth Keeble, London
John L Kellett
Dorothy Kent, Oadby (formerly Ripon)
Dave & Pauline Kenyon, Doncaster
John Kernahan, Aberdeen
D W Kershaw
G A King, Cannington, Ontario
J E H Kingdon, Harrogate
Mrs C J Kinloch
Trudie Kintish, Manchester
Kirkby in Malhamdale
  United VA Primary School
Harold Knee, Leeds
John & Lesley Knight, Swanley
Paul Knight
S B Knott
Erna E Kritzinger, Hebden

Chris Lackey
Mrs K M Lamb
E Lane, Radcliffe on Trent
Mrs M E Lang
Charlotte Rose Larder
S Larter, Grande Prairie, Alberta
Lynne Lashbrooke, Sherborne, Dorset
David Laughton, Carrigaline
Peter Lawrenson
Mrs E M Leckie
Ann Lee
Dave Leedham, Halifax
N Leefe, Bramhope
D A Leeming, Barwick in Elmet
Mrs M A Lees
Mrs C Lemmon
Peter Leveridge, Eaton, Norwich
Eileen Lewis, Woulpit, Suffolk
Leyburn County Primary School
P Lightfoot, Otley
M E Lindley, Shepley
Dr & Mrs P A Linley, Baildon
T V Linley, Leeds
Peter J Little MBE, Rotherham
Chris & Maureen Lock,
  Sutton Coldfield
Baroness Lockwood
Mr & Mrs P Lockwood, Leeds
Mrs M Lomas
Mrs V Lonsdale, Scalby, Scarboro'
L & W Lord
George Luffman, Ilkley
Mrs C M Lumb, Knaresborough
Miss D Lumb
Ray Lumb, Cleckheaton

Elizabeth Macalister
John & Edna Macfadyen,
  Highcliffe-on-Sea
Nancy McGregor, Redmire
Margaret R McLagan
Sophie Kathryn Mair
Mrs B L Mann
Elisabeth Mannering, Freshwater Bay
James G Marchbank, Dumfries
J Markham
Keith Marris, Kingston upon Hull
Mr & Mrs A O Marshall, Whitby
Capt G Marshall OBE, Pocklington
Ray Marshall, Mirfield
Mrs N Marston (in memory of a
  dear husband, Stan)
Charles Martin, Haslemere
D Martin, Hullbridge
J D Martin
Mrs M H Martin
Rex Martin, Pateley Bridge
Miss W M Martin, Bainbridge
Rev Canon Mrs R D Martineau,
  Gildersome
Alan Masheder, Darlington
N R R Mason, Saltford
Mrs Pam Mather, Mayfield
Dorothy Maude, Threshfield
Maureen, Doncaster
N S Maw, Almondbury
Cedric A Maxey

Melbecks Gunnerside Methodist
  Primary School
Mell-Williams, Barrow, Suffolk
Paul & Heather Mercer
Mrs G F Meredith
Mr & Mrs G E Messent
Mrs P C Metcalfe, Harrogate
H W Midgley, Guernsey
Miss M Midgley

Mr & Mrs A H Mills, Birstwith
Dr Derek Mills, Melrose
David Milner, Knaresborough
Miss Elsie Milner
C G R Milnes, Bradford
Mrs A C Minchin, Loughborough
Karen & Ciara Minnitt, Walkden
Mason & Shena Minnitt,
  Kirkby Lonsdale
Robin Minnitt, Askrigg
William & Helen Minnitt,
  North Marston
Mrs Celia Mitchell, Carlisle
David Mitchell, Fleet
D R Moad
Elizabeth M Moody,
  Burley-in-Wharfedale
Christine & Martin Moore
John Mordy, Bramhope
Margaret Morris, Upper Westwood
Mrs K G Moss
Mrs Mowat
A Muckalt, Kendal
Roy Mundy, Clapham
Ian Murden, Davyhulme, Manchester
Jim Murray
Marion & Alan Murray
Miss S P & Miss J E Mutlow, Torquay
Enid & Laurence Myers, Harrogate

Ann Naylor, Whitley Bay
Iris Newby
Pat & Roy Newton, Sutton-in-Craven
Robert & Judith Nicholls
Ms A Nightingale
Mrs M Nixon
Dr T C Noble, Sedbergh

Mary O' Donnell, Harrogate
Mrs S M Ogden
F, C & E Ogilvie, Settle
Keith & Brenda Oglesby
Ann Oldacre, Doncaster
Joyce E Oldfield, Standish
June Oldham, Ilkley
Mrs G Oldroyd, Sandal
Olicana History Society, Ilkley
S D Oliver, Hoo Bears, Kidderminster
Mr & Mrs G Ong, N Featherstone
Norah Osgerby, Sheffield
C M Overton
Kenneth Owens, Northampton

Dr Michael I Padgett
Prof Stephen Padgett
Audrey & Brian Page, Hull
Miss Denise Page
Dr & Mrs J F Page, Earlswood
Christopher Pain, St Sulpice de
  Cognac, France
Lewis Pannell, Birmingham
Harry D Parker, Linton, Wetherby
M S & L Parker, Sedbusk, Hawes
Mr & Mrs Parkin, Blackpool
Jane A Parkinson
Nevil Parkinson
Gary & Hazel Passmore, New Marske
E J Paternoster, Colchester
Kenneth Payne, Leeds
Malcolm W Payne, Port Carling,
  Ontario
Raymond Payne, Great Holm
Bernice & Jerry Pearlman, Leeds
Debbie Pearlman, Wheathamstead
K Pearlman-Shaw, Leeds
Kate, Jonathon & Mark
  Pearlman-Shaw, Leeds

L & S Pears, Newbold Verdon
A R Pemberton, Settle
Terry Perkins
D C Phillips
Barbara Pickersgill, Leeds
Jane Pickett, Frettenham
Geoff Piercy, Penyfford, Chester
Patrick Pilcher, Scaynes Hill
D Pimp
Mrs P Pinder
Mrs Anne Plant, Shatterford
L Plews
Mark William Pounder
J D Prest
D D Preston, Ilkley
Carolyn & Peter Prior, Stourbridge
Mrs E Pritchard
W Procter
Mrs Freda Proctor, Eldwick
W E Proctor

Mr & Mrs C J Quickfall,
 Tunbridge Wells
A Quigley

Blanche L Race, Bradley
Alison Raw, Darlington
J D Raw, Bingley
Mrs S M Read
Mrs E Reading, Pontefract
Colin Redfern, Brindle
Corinne Redfern
Alan & Ruth Redgwick
Mrs Anne Reid, Sough
Jean Reinsch, Grassington
Miss M Relton, Hull
Sylvia Render, Worcester
Mrs J Rennardson, Willerby
Anne & Malcolm Renshaw, Selside
M Rhodes, New House, Gayle
J Stuart Rhodes, Wistaston, Crewe
William Henry Richards,
 Newcastle under Lyme
Ian Richardson, Beverley
Jane Iveson Richardson,
 Seaton Sluice
Stuart Richardson, Dewsbury
Ron Richford
Pauline M Riley
Alec Patrick Riordan (in memory)
Elisabeth Roberts, Sidcup
Ian & Diane Roberts, Hazlemere
Jane Roberts
Jean & Selwyn Roberts, Grimsby
Mr & Mrs B Robertshaw, Ivybridge
T J Robertshaw
B Robinson, Bradford
Mrs G Robinson, Halifax
Mary Robinson, Horsforth
Mrs P Robinson
Sheila Robinson
Sylvia M Robinson
Thomas Michael Robinson
 (11/12/28 - 15/12/95)
J Roper, Blackpool
Michael J Rogers, Ferrybridge
Margaret Rooker, Halifax
Steve Rowley
Ruth and Ann, Harrogate

William B Sabey
Mrs Joan Salter
Mark Sandamas, Barnoldswick
Gail Sanderson, Aviemore
John Keith Sandy, Skelmanthorpe
Mr & Mrs J Saunders, Horsforth
Bryan Scaife, Ingleby Barwick

John Scarborough, Hebden Brdige
H & V Schaufelberger
Mrs M Schofield
Anne Sebastian, West Riding
W Secker, Dewsbury
Martin Seeber, Harrogate
Mrs B Sellers
Settlebeck High School, Sedbergh
Elizabeth Seymour, Steeton
Ray & Doreen Shadrake, Cheltenham
Derek Shaw, Bramham
John Sheard, Bolton Abbey
Joan Shearer, Rotherham
Anna Sheasby, Addingham
Margaret Shooter
Mrs D Sichi
Andrew P Siddle, Hull
E Charles Simpson,
 Burley in Wharfedale
Skipton Building Society
Andrew Slade, Bedford
Matthew Slade, Didcot
The Slater Family (in memory of
 a dear Dad and Grandad)
Ken & Mary Smallpage, Leyburn
Margaret Smart, Darlington
Mrs C J Smee
David Smith, Ilkley
David & Joyce Smith, Harrogate
J D Smith
Jean M Smith, Benfleet
Joan & Tom Smith & Family, Ontario
M Smith, Stockton-on-Tees
Peter & Beverley Smith, Halesowen
The Smith Family (in memory of
 a dear Dad and Grandad)
A Smithies, Knaresborough
Miss D Smithson, Ilkley
Edward Smithson, Bardsey
Geoff Snook, Southampton
Mrs Jessie Soar, Rawdon
Margaret Sowden, Harrogate
I M Speight, Bradford
The Sprays
Geoff & Jill Spring, Sherington
Mrs Anne Staniforth
Mrs M Stansfield
Jean Staples, Doncaster
R W Stark, York
S Stead, Yeadon
Dick Stokes, Harrogate
Chris Stone, Ilford, Essex
V M Stone
J A Stott, Bolton
Mr & Mrs James Stott, Bolton
K R & J M Stott, East Witton
Roger Stott
Philip John Streather, Harrogate
Ann & John Stroud, Newport,
 Australia
Stuart, Leeds
Harry Stubbs, Brotherton
Kevin Stubbs, Romsey
Robin & Susan Stubbs,
 Apperley Bridge
A J Sutcliffe
Arthur & Angela Summerfield,
 Sutton-under-Whitestonecliffe
Daphne Sutherland, Burton in Lonsdale
Roy & Doreen Swarster,
 Wheathampstead
Herman de Swart
J M & G A Sykes, High Casterton

Mrs K H Tasker, Gainsborough
Andrew R Tate, Osmotherley
D E Taylor

Eileen Taylor, Cottingham
E R Taylor, Knaresborough
Jane & Geoffrey Taylor, Litton
Mary Taylor
Mrs E M Temple
Benjamin Edward Ternent, Cullercoats
Mr & Mrs K R Thieme
J P Thomas, Smeeth, Ashford
Mrs S A Thomas, Nairn
Faith Thompson, Garstang
Adrianne Thomson, Timble
Mrs E Thomson
Mr & Mrs C Thorpe
D G & L D Thwaites
Frank Thyssen, Venlo, Netherlands
Rev Kenneth Tibbetts, Prestatyn
Derek Tidmarsh
Jean Mary Tilleard, Wrose
Mr & Mrs R Tilley, Ilkley
Michael & Barbara Tobin,
 Northampton
Kathleen Topley, Nottingham
Aline & Buci Torday, Matterdale
K Towler, Leeds
Maureen Treacy, Duston
Caitlin Turner
David Turner, Brentwood
Mrs H Turner, Burley-in-Wharfedale
Mrs J Turner
S Turner
Maurice Twinham
Sidney Twinham
Hazel Tyrrell

Mrs M O Uden

Louise Van Cappellen, St Bees
Reg & Jean Vickers, Bradford

D M Wade
Rita & Michael Wadsworth,
 Todmorden
Carolyn & Dan Wagner, Columbia, USA
Richard & Leaghie Wainwright, Litton
Mrs C M Walker, York
C Richard Walker, Liversedge
Ms Anne Wallin, Scarborough
Anthony Walsh, Rawdon
Miss I P Walsh
Jean B Walton
David & Carole Warburton
Mrs J Ward
Mrs Muriel Ward, Irby, Wirral
Mrs G M Warwick
Janet Warnick, Southport
C Warriner, Cleveland
G M Warwick, Everton
Mary Waterhouse
J K Waterworth
Alan & Shirley Watkinson, Hawes
Stephen P Watkinson (In Memory)
Stephen Watling, Little Baddow
E Lucie Watson, Howden
Mrs I D Watson, Sidmouth
John Watson, Bradford
N J & J A Watson
R A Watson, Scarborough
Dorothy Watson-Grigs, Edinburgh
Barbara Watts
R & J Waxham
Mrs H F Waycott
Mr & Mrs R J Wearing, Bolton-le-Sands
Vera Weatherley
C Webb, London
K Webb, Sheffield
Simon Webb, Bainbridge
Terence Edward Webb

E H & I Webster, Astley Village
Diane Welburn, Hull
Mrs Sue Wells
S M Western
Christopher J Whatmough, Rochdale
Mrs A Wheeler, Woodford Green
Mrs S M Whincup
Basil & Sandra White, Boston Spa
C M White
Mrs M L White
Peter & Jane White, Boston Spa
Raymond F White
Mr & Mrs B Whitehouse, Ilkley
Mrs M Whitney, Seacroft
David Whittaker
Dr M W Whittaker
John & June Wilcock & Family,
 West Riding
John & Mary Wiles, Tylers Green
D Wiley
Jill Wilkinson, Wimborne
Betty M Willcox, Droitwich Spa
Barbara Williams, Dhahran,
 Saudi Arabia
D A Williams, Aldershot
Pamela Anne Williams
Trudie Williams, Newbury
Mrs V Williams
Charles Williamson, King's Lynn
Mark & Ian Willingham, Airton
J E K Willson, Addingham
D M Wilmot, Bath
Alan G Wilson, Brampton, Hunts
Clive Wilson, Harrogate
Mr & Mrs D Wilson, Doncaster
D & L V Wilson, Ossett
Jack Wilson
Mrs V Wilson
Peter & Ruth Winch, Reading
J R Winn
David Witt, Bolton
Hilda Witt, Leeds
Richard Witt
Derek & Maureen Wood, Huddersfield
Eileen & Harold Wood, Leeds
H E Wood, Leeds
H M Wood
Mrs M Wood
Mrs E F Woodhead
Linton Woodman, Addingham
Ron Woodhouse, Rotherham
Eileen Woodley
S M Woolnough, Ilkley
Norman & Joyce Wordsworth, Eastby
Vera & John Worledge, Northampton
Eric Georgina Wormald, Grassington
J Wormald, Selby
Jane Worrall of Hensall
Miss Worsley-Taylor, Bashall Eaves
Rev J G Wragg, Filey
Joy Wrathall, Nottingham
M J Wren
Mrs B Wright, Farnsfield
Brett Allen Wright, Huddersfield
Chris Wright & Sue, Gargrave
Martyn Wright
Mrs Miram Wright, Grassington
Tony Andrew Wright, Huddersfield
C M Wrigley

Olive & Donald Yates
Alan Yeo, Cambridge
A G & D I Young, Birmingham
Mrs M W I Yule, Matlock